NOTES

NOTES

NOTES

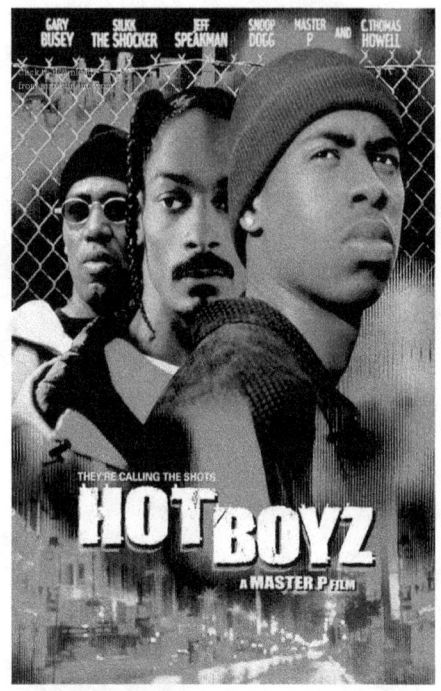

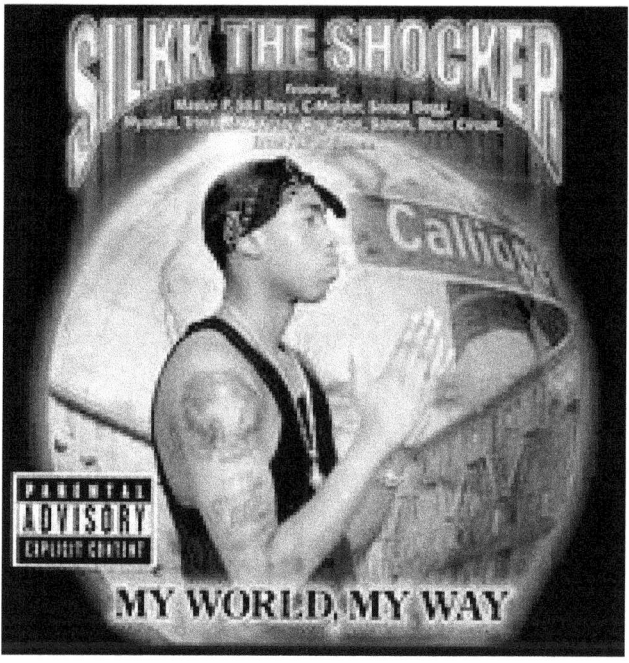

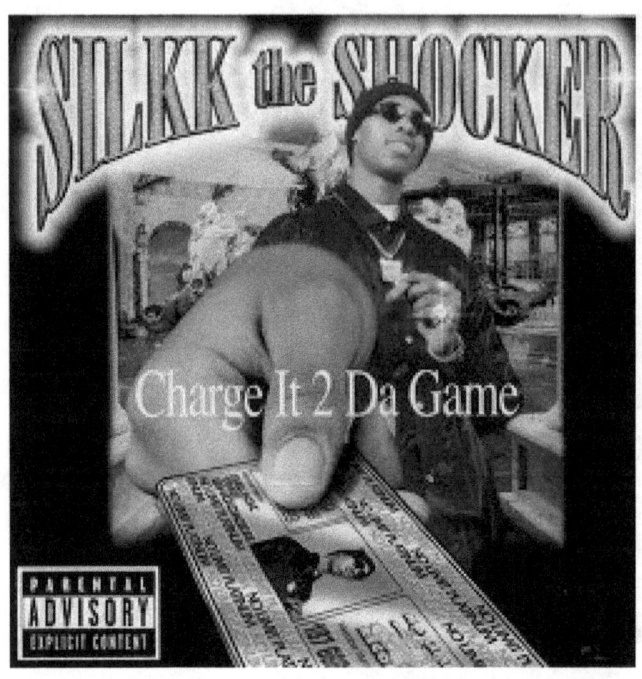

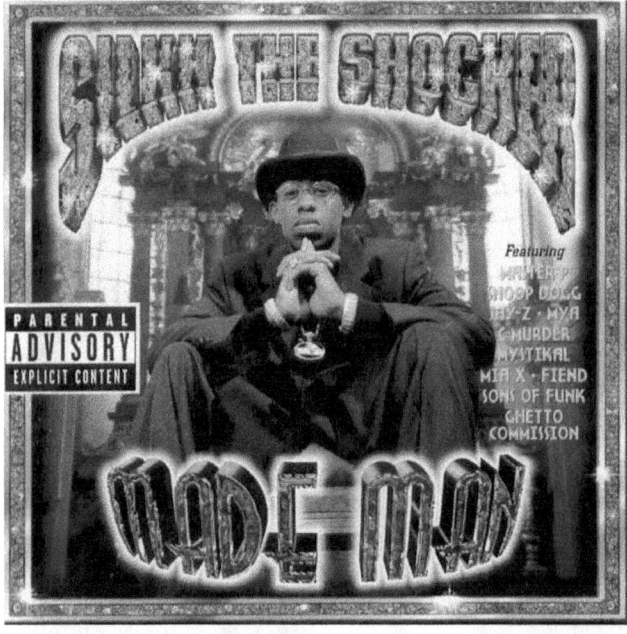

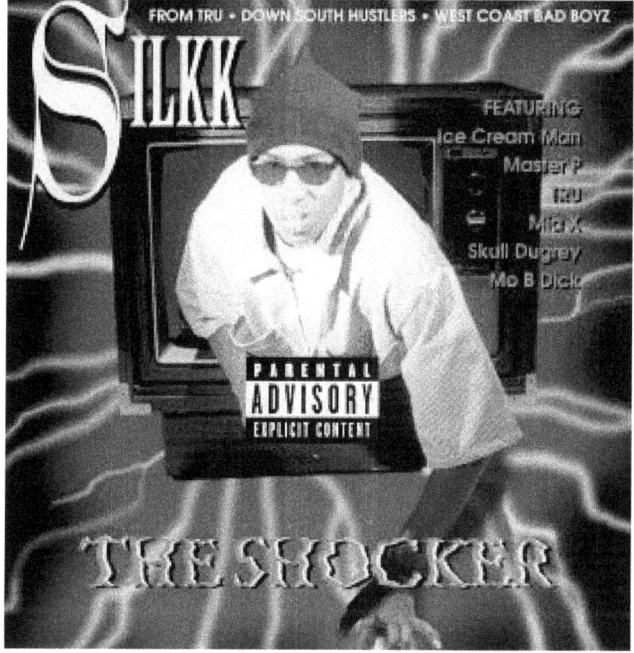

143 • PAVED: THE NAVIGATED GUIDE TO SUCCEEDING IN THE MUSIC INDUSTRY

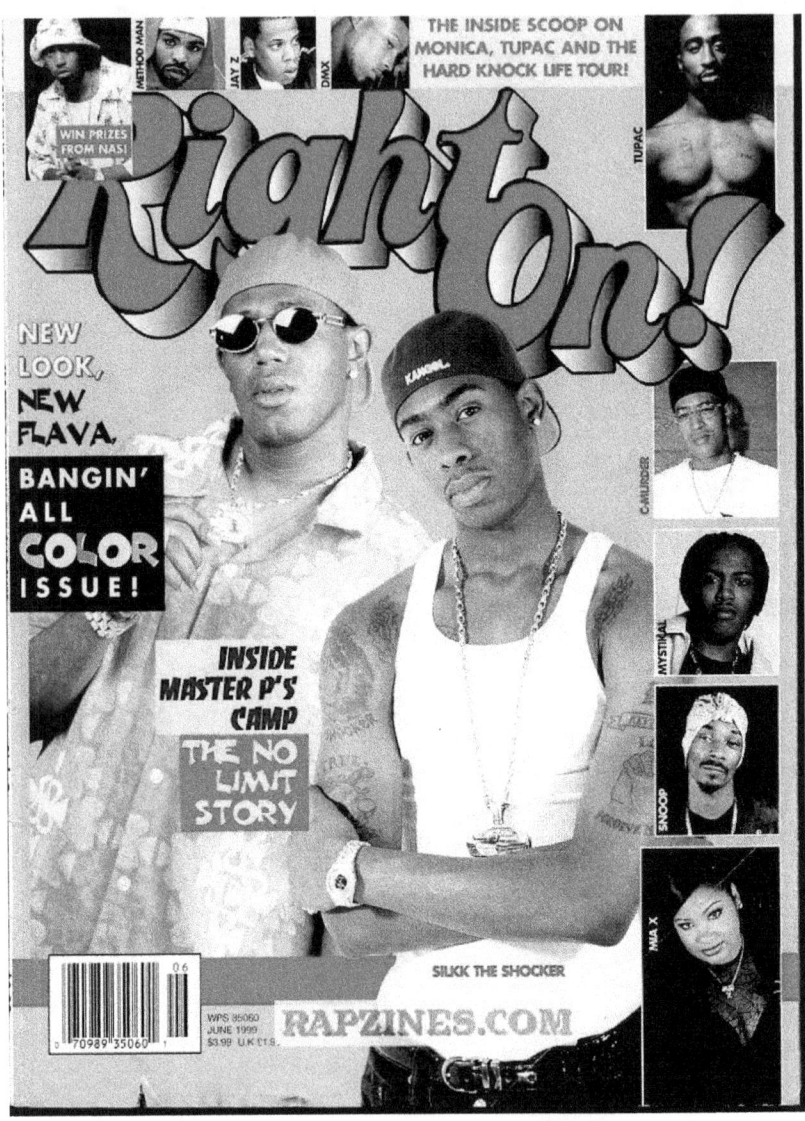

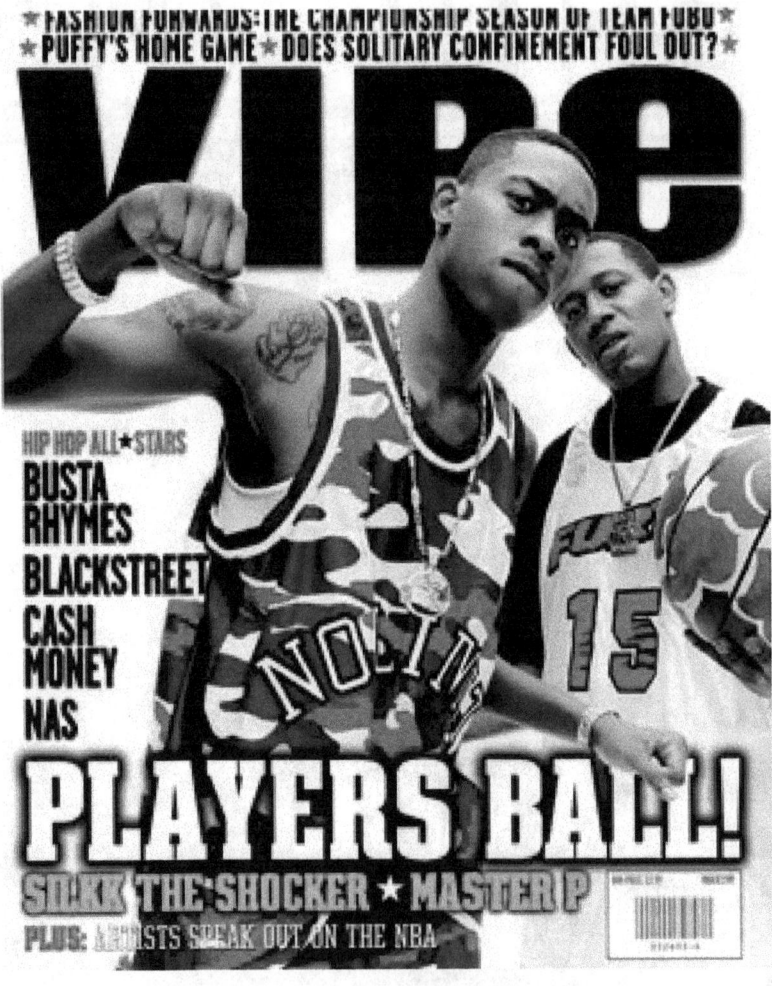

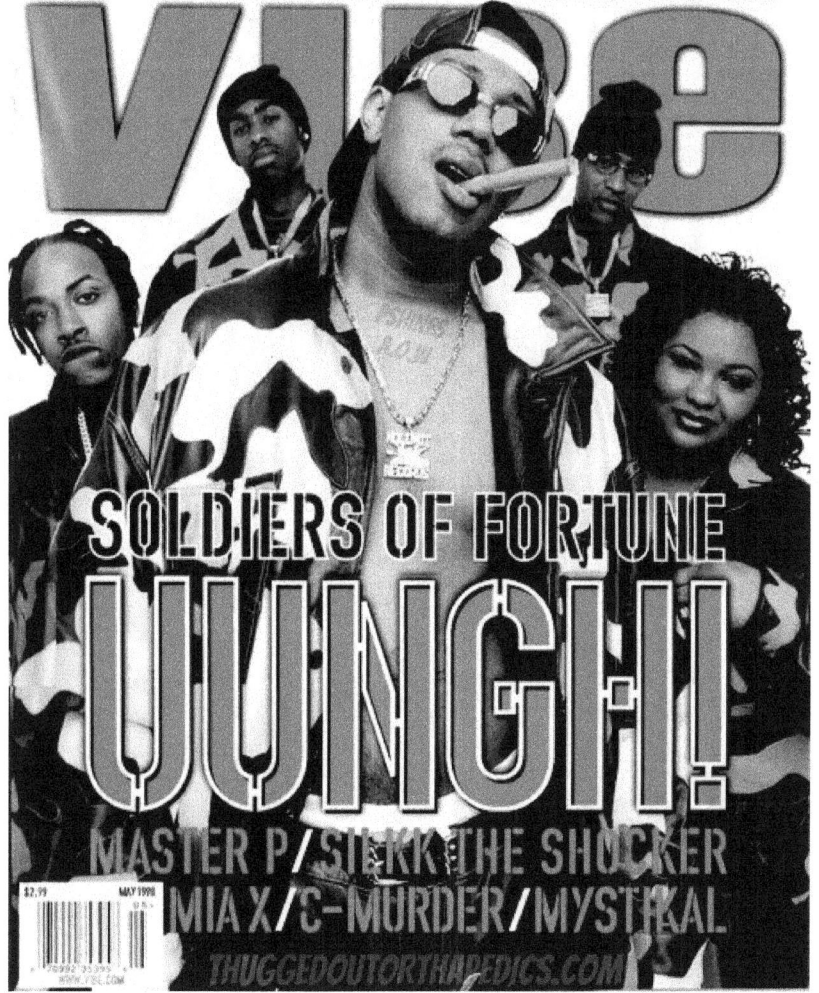

I would like to send a SPECIAL THANK YOU to:

To all my family and friends My Dad, My Mom, My Aunt Marie because when I was growing up, she never said I couldn't & always said I could, when so many counted me out! My whole entire family, cause no matter what, good or bad; at the end of the day we family. T. Miles, No Limit Boyz, Champ, Jimmie Motorbike Mike , my rib Ju, Joan, Judy ,uncle Joe uncle,Jerry all My godson,my nieces,nephews and cousins. Thank you to Pastor Mark for the wisdom & always being a brother and friend; Pastor Desiree Jackson and family, Jianni, King, VJ, V'Elijah, J'Isaiah, Valor, Micah.. Thank you to my friends, Curtis Burton, Big Clint, Ricky Waters, SHo Nuff, Joq , Bro Kenny, Chance , Rich Goldberg, Bubba, Manny Street, Big Boy, DJ Ominaya, Superstar Jay, Sway, Ed Lover, To-To ,DJ Holiday, , Jimmi the Jewler, Savanah, Jack Thriller, Roy, J.O, Mean green, NBA Ent. Thank Roger Raymond for everything and a special shout out to Gifted Johnson for all your help. A Special Thank You and Big Shout-Outs to T. Church for all you Tricia Lee for everything and then some. Special shout goes to my fam my brother Master P for sacrafice and hard work and huslte that help so many, My sister Germany, My brother Corey Miller cant wait til you free, Rest in Peace to My brother Kevin Miller forever motivates me. We family no matter what people may Think Love you all. Plus I am Sure I missed Alot of people and if id did you know all love and I got you next time I know I am forgetting so many but all love going to you and Thank You to each and every person who supported me and contributed to my growth; if you added anything, even if was just a word.

I salute EVERY Artist , Dj , Program Director, Radio Personality , Street Team & Fan in cities across the world. Thank you for the bottom of my heart and I appreciate each and every one of you named and not named. This music business wouldn't be still thriving and so many wouldn't be prospering from if, it wasn't for y'all. I don't do anything unless it has a purpose or it is to better someone or something. If it wasn't for that, I would just sit quietly and mind my own business and live my life. BUT, with power and knowledge come great responsibility and sometimes that comes with even greater burdens. I am sure the ones before me felt a great responsibility and they pushed through paving the way for others to have it better.

Too $hort, Nas, Big Pun, Camron, DJ Quik, West Side Connection, Dogg Pound, Ice Cube, Q-tip, Cypress Hill, Nelly, Lil John, Slick Rick, Dr. Dre, Bone Thugs-N-Harmony, Scarface, Common, Capone & Norega, Jermaine Dupree, Ice-T, DMX, State Property, Salt-N-Pepa, Eminem, Most Def, New Edition, Outcast, Aaliyah, No Limit Soldiers, Timbaland, Total, R. Kelly, Ludacris, Trick Daddy, UGK, Mystikal, and The Roots

THANK YOU...to the ones that are now are paving the way for the next generation....

The Game, Big Sean, Bow-Wow, Trina , Fat Joe, Remy Martin, Plies , DJ Khaled, Drake, 50 Cent, Kanye West, French Montana, Meek Mills, Wale, Anderson Pak, Wiz Kalifa , Kanye West, Lacrae, Young Jeezy, Rick Ross, Gucci Mane, Young Dolph, Ludacris, Joey Bad Ass, Kendrick Lamar, Asap Rocky, Asap Ferg, Nick Cannon, Lupe Fiasco, Tech N9ne, Logic, Chance the Rapper, Yo Gotti, Fab, Kodak Black, 21 Savage, Ty Dolla$, Post Malone, Lil Durk, Dave East, Pusha T, School Boy Q, Migos, New No Limit Artist, Party Next door, Tyga, Wiz Kalifa, Fetty Wap, Mac Mill, TI, Dej Loaf, Nicki Minaj, Romeo, Blac N mild, Zatoven, Big K.R.I.T, Kevin Gates, Lil Boosie, BoB, KCamp, King Miller, The Weekend, Casey Veggies, Syaridakid; and PNB

Hip Hop introduced me to music and music introduced me to world of music, which also brings me to a THANK YOU to:

Michael Jackson, Beyoncé, Taylor swift, Celine Dion, Lauryn Hill, T, Blink 182, Justin Bieber, Byson Tiller, Steve Ayoki, Rihanna , Usher, Garth Brooks, Cold Play, One Direction, Chris Brown, J-Lo, Toni Braxton, Whitney Houston, Justin Timberlake, Janet Jackson, Black Eyed Peas,

Russell Simmons , Shante Dias , Motown, No Limit, Cash Money, Rap-A-Lot, Sick Wid It, Def Jam, Sony, Priority, So-So Def, Bad Boy, and all The Labels.

My thanks to the ones mentioned aren't based on who likes who; on opinions; how much they did or didn't do; or how much they sold, but the for the sole reason and purpose to acknowledge their contribution to the ever growing music industry.

Silkk "The Shocker" Miller Thank you's

First and foremost, I want to thank God and Jesus my Lord and Savior. For without HIM nothing is possible! Thank you for giving me strength, wisdom, mercy and for continuously watching over me. May you get all the glory!

I must admit at first my Thank You was going to be this....."I want to Thank all my family and friends who supported me; helped me; and motivated me. I want to thank everyone who paved the way for music thus far. Thank you to the past, present and future musician and executives. I am truly thankful because of you this business has given people hope, jobs and opportunities. Thank you & God Bless".

Well, after realizing that would be an injustice of what it is, and knowing it's much bigger than that, there is so much more that deserved to be acknowledged. It is important to have the knowledge of what perseverance is in this business.

With that being said, I pay homage and say THANK YOU to the ones that paved the way before me (Just to mention a few)....

NWA, 2PAC, Puffy, Naughty By Nature, Dougie Fresh, Heavy D and the Boyz, Lil Kim, Craig Mack, Foxy Brown, Queen Latifah, Slick Rick, Ghetto Boys, 2 Live Crew, Whodunit, Marley, Pete Rock and CL Smooth, The LOX, Dana Dane, Busta Rhymes, MC Hammer, Chubb Rock, Steady B, Monie Love, House of Pain, Mac Dre, 2 Live Crew, Arrested Development, Public Enemy, Sugarhill Gang, The Fugees, Digital Underground, Cool C, Frankie Smith,Naughty By Nature, Red Man, MC Lyte, Onyx, Sir Mix-A-Lot, Tone-Loc, Nate Dogg, Compton's Most Wanted, Dj Jazzy Jeff, Fresh Prince, Mobb Deep, The Pharchyde, The Beastie Boys, 3rd Base, KRS-One, Eric B. & Rakim, De La Soul, EPMD, BDP,A Tribe Called Quest, Ultramagnetic MC's, and the Jungle Brothers, Wu Tang Clan, Notorious BIG, Jay Z, Snoop Dogg, E40,

About Silkk "The Shocker" Miller

Born Vyshonne King Miller in the late spring of 1976 in New Orleans, Louisiana, since infancy Silkk learned that life wouldn't be picture perfect unless he was holding the camera or painting the picture himself. Growing up below poverty point in the 3rd ward Calliope Projects located in Central City New Orleans, an urban housing development that infamously gained notoriety for having extremely high violence and an ever growing crime rate, Silkk knew that he wanted something more and needed a way out. That way out would come at the young age of 13 by way of his older brother Percy (Master P), who moved out west to Richmond, California to build a better way of life for his family. This move would be the starting point of a journey that would forever change Silkk's life.

Out West, Life for Silkk was different than what he'd left behind in New Orleans. Learning the ropes of hard work and business ownership hands on with his brother who started a record store named No Limit Records, would prove to serve a greater purpose for the road that was ahead. Building up a solid work ethic not only molded a genius like mindset for him but also taught him how to navigate throughout the system. Silkk would embody the wider spectrum of greatness early on in his career by staying focused and driven on his goals. This process would prove to be the befitting key to the many doors of success that approached him swiftly. From trials to triumph and back again, Silkk has stayed prepared and has never wavered from his ethical prowess as a gifted Artist.

All of the hard work that Silkk has put into his dreams would spark instant inspiration for the masses. They too could change their circumstances by staying determined and motivated as he did. His rags to riches story serves as the perfect backdrop to self aspiration, from projects to platinum selling records Silkk has grounded himself amongst the pioneers and will continue to push the mold for generations to come.

- Widget : A widget is a stand-alone application that can be embedded into third-party sites by any user on a page where the user has rights of authorship (e.g. a webpage, blog, or profile on a social media site). Widgets allow users to turn personal content into dynamic web apps that can be shared on just about any website. Widgets may be viewed as downloadable applications that look and act like traditional apps but are implemented using web technologies, including JavaScript, Flash, HTML and CSS.

- Work Registration Form : Declaration of a musical work, including the title, duration and shareholder information such as percentages related to its creators (writer, composer) and to the publisher.

- Work for Hire : A work for hire is an exception to the general rule that the person who creates a work is the legally recognized author of that work. Under US copyright law and in some other jurisdictions, if a work is "made for hire", the employer, not the employee is considered the legal author.

- Writer Share : The percentage of ownership in a work attributable to the author and/or composer.

- Trademark : A trademark is a distinctive sign or symbol used by an individual, business organization or legal entity to identify a work, a product or a service, in order to distinguish itself from other entities. A trademark is a type of intellectual property and typically a name, word, phrase, logo, symbol, design or image.

- Transformative Use : This refers to the fair use defense particularly in judicial decisions relating to parody and satire. Transformative use is cited as a reason which exempts uses "for the purposes of caricature, parody or pastiche". Although these uses are not defined, they allow users to reuse elements of previous works for their own creative or transformative purpose.

- Viral marketing : Viral marketing describes strategies that encourage individuals to pass on a marketing message to others, creating the potential for exponential growth in the message's exposure and influence. Like viruses, such strategies take advantage of rapid multiplication to explode the message to thousands, or to millions. The goal of successful viral-marketing programs is to identify individuals with high social networking potential (SNP) and create viral messages that appeal to this segment of the population and have a high probability of being taken by another competitor. Viral marketing has been referred to as "word-of-mouth," "creating a buzz," "leveraging the media" and "network marketing."

- Web 2.0 : This term is commonly associated with web applications that facilitate interactive information sharing, interoperability and user-centered features. Examples of Web 2.0 applications include web-based communities and applications, hosted services, social-networking sites, video-sharing sites, wikis, blogs and mashup sites. A Web 2.0 website allows its users to interact with other users or to change website content, in contrast to non-interactive websites where users are limited to the passive viewing of information that is provided to them.

- Webcast : A webcast is a media file distributed over the Internet using streaming media technology to distribute an audio or video message to many simultaneous listeners/viewers. A webcast may either be distributed live or on demand. Essentially, webcasting is "broadcasting" over the Internet.

- Small Rights : This refers to the bundle of rights in a musical work comprising performance, communication and reproduction rights (mechanical, synchronization and print). The term 'small rights' normally refers to performing rights that are not grand rights.

- Social Networking Sites : Social networking websites focus on building and reflecting social networks or social relations among people, such as those who share interests and/or activities. A social network site normally consists of a user profile, his or her social links, and a variety of additional services used to communicate with other users of the service.

- Sound Exchange : The US organization, affiliated with the RIAA, which licenses and collects royalties for some digital performances of sound recordings (i.e. on web radio or websites with music). www.soundexchange.com

- Sound Recording : In essence, a sound recording is the "sound carrier" a generic term used for any technology (media) that allows recording to be stored.

- Streaming : Streaming is the act of sending and receiving content in a compressed form over the Internet. With streaming video or streaming media, a Web user does not have to wait to download a file to play it. Instead, the media is sent in a continuous stream of data and is played as it arrives.

- Sub-Publishing Agreement : A foreign publisher that represents the entire catalogue or individual copyrights of another publisher (the "original publisher") in another country. Sub-publishers generally do not have any ownership share and for the most part focus on administration, although creative exploitation may also be undertaken by foreign sub-publishers.

- Synchronization (SYNCH) Right : The sync right is the right to authorize the recording of a musical work onto the sound track of an audio/visual work (film, television program, music video, video game, commercial). A synchronization license is needed for a song to be reproduced and songwriters and publishers receive royalties for sync rights.

and/or sound recordings. This may also include the management of rights for other revenue- generating intellectual property, such as logos, names, images etc.

• Ringtone/Ringback : A ringtone is the sound (or sounds) that a cellular phone plays to warn the subscriber that there is an incoming call. A ringback is the sound (or sounds) that a cellular telephone plays to let the listener know that an outgoing call is being made. More often than not, ringtones as well as ringback tones are excerpts of a musical work.

• Royalty : A sum paid to copyright owners for the sale or use of their musical works or other subject matter.

• Royalty Participation Agreement :A contract between a copyright owner (i.e. a composer) and a third party (i.e. an investor, producer or non-writing band member). In these contracts, normally the copyright owner agrees to share a percentage of specified royalty streams for a specific period of time under certain terms with others who may have contributed to the success of the copyright, even though these others did create the work(s). The parties have no ownership share in the copyright of the work(s) in question. The royalty payable under these contracts are commonly referred to as the "Loyalty Royalty".

• Sample (1) : The random sample method of logging the communication and public performances of a musical work (i.e.radio performance logs used by PROs).

• Sample (2) : As in "sampling a record". A creative appropriation of a section, piece or element of a copyrighted sound recording and the underlying musical composition. In most cases, the "sample" must be cleared with the copyright owners (i.e.: record la-bel and music publisher), to avoid future infringement claims.

• Shareholder : In the context of music creators, an author, composer, arranger or publisher that owns a percentage of a work.

- Publishing Agreement : A legal contract between a composer/lyricist (author)/songwriter and a publisher.

- Publishing Administrator : A third-party publisher that – for a fixed term –controls all licensing and the collection of publishing revenue streams on behalf of a composer or copyright owner.

- Publisher Share : The share of revenues granted to the music publisher via a publishing contract, depending on the type of publishing agreement (i.e. songwriter, co-publishing, sub-publishing, administration. Normally, the publisher's share can never exceed 50%. Depending on the type of publishing agreement, a publisher may acquire an "ownership share" in the copyrights for a period of time, including in perpetuity , this being the traditional and most common basis of an agreement.

- Reciprocal Agreement: A reciprocal agreement is a two-way agreement whereby the obligations assumed and imposed by two parties are mutual and conditional upon one party assuming the same obligations as the other.

- Recoup/Recoupment : Record companies make monetary advances to artists to fund the production and marketing costs of producing a recording, and for concert tours. The record companies then "recoup" these funds from the proceeds of record sales, Recoupment is a common practice in the music industry of claiming an advance provided to an artist back from that artist.

- Reproduction Right : Under the Copyright Act, the reproduction right gives the copyright owner the exclusive right to authorize the reproduction of music (usually called "mechanical licensing") and in films, TV programs and other audio-visual productions ("synchronization licensing").

- Rights Management : The comprehensive, overall administration of copyrights owned by an individual or company, and the resulting revenue streams that deal with copyrighted musical works and/or sound recordings. This may also include the management of rights for other revenue- generating intellectual property, such as logos, names, images etc.

- Override : A royalty paid to producers of sound recordings based on the sales of recordings. It is normally a negotiated percentage (usually 1 to 3 points) which is paid by the record label to the producer, either in addition to the Artist's royalty or taken from the Artist's royalty points.

- P2P (Peer to Peer): A sharing and delivery of user-specified files among groups of people who are logged onto a file- sharing network. Peer-to-peer (P2P) networking eliminates the need for central servers, allowing all computers to communicate and share resources as equals. Music file sharing, instant messaging and other popular net-work applications rely on P2P technology.

- Performing / Communication Right : One of the rights in the "bundle of rights" (see Small Rights) that comprises the copyright in a musical work. Specifically, this relates to the public performance of copyrighted musical works (broadcast, live performance) and the communication by telecommunication of musical works (cable TV transmissions, Internet, mobile, satellite, etc.).

- Performing Rights Organization (PRO) : An organization that administers the performing rights associated with a musical work, on behalf of composers, lyricists, songwriters and music publishers.

- Perpetuity : This term usually means payments with no definitive end.

- Posthumous work : A work which is published for the first time (or, for certain types of works, performed or delivered in public for the first time) after the author's death.

- Private Copying : Copying for personal use, a pre-recorded musical work or a per-formers' performances of a musical work onto a blank medium, such as an audio tape, cassette, or CD-R.

- Public Domain (PD) : Works are in the public domain if they are not covered by intellectual property rights at all, if the intellectual property rights have expired and/or if the intellectual property rights are forfeited.

- Master Use License : Is a license to make reproductions of master recordings.

- Mechanical Royalty : Mechanical royalties are amounts paid to a songwriter or composer for the reproduction of a work thru CD etc.

- Moral Rights : Rights an author retains over the integrity of a work and the right to be named as its author even after sale or transfer of the copyright. As the primary owners, creators of musical or other works may transfer their economic interest in these works to third parties (e.g., to another individual or company). However, creators may not transfer or assign their moral rights – although they may choose not to exercise them

- Most Favored Nations (MFN) : In the context of music industry agreements, an MFN clause provides that an amount, a definition, or another aspect of a contractual relationship (such as license or royalty fees) will be computed or defined in at least as favorable a manner as the computation or definition given to one or more third parties.

- Music Publisher : A music publisher is responsible for ensuring that songwriters and composers receive payment when their compositions are commercially used.

- Music Supervisor : A music supervisor is the person in charge of placing music in films, TV shows, advertising and video games.

- Musical Work : Any work of music or musical composition, with or without words.

- Orphan Works : Works under copyright for which the owner(s) cannot be identified or located (i.e. because the record company or music publisher has gone out of business).

- Override : A royalty paid to producers of sound recordings based on the sales of recordings. It is normally a negotiated percentage (usually 1 to 3 points) which is paid by the record label to the producer, either in addition to the Artist's royalty or taken from the Artist's royalty points.

- Indie (Independent): Normally refers to a band or performer not affiliated with or owned by a major label.

- Intellectual Property : A form of creative endeavor that can be protected through a copyright, trademark, patent, industrial design or integrated circuit topography.

- Interpolated Work : A song that is not written expressly for an audio-visual production but is taken from an outside source (e.g., recording) and used within that production.

- IPI #: Interested Parties Information is an international, CISAC classification system that identifies a musical work and its shareholders, using a unique number.

- ISRC : The International Standard Recording Code is an international identification system for sound recordings and music videos. Each ISRC is a unique and permanent identifier for a specific recording that can be permanently encoded into a product as its digital "fingerprint". Encoded ISRCs provide the basic means to automatically identify recordings for royalty payments.

- Library of Congress (part of Copyright Registration) : A federal cultural institution in the US. Located in Washington D.C., it receives copies of every book, print, and piece of music registered in the country.

- License: A legal agreement granting someone permission to use a work for certain purposes or under certain conditions. A license does not change the ownership of the copyright.

- Mash-up : A mash-up is a song or composition created by blending or mixing two or more songs together, normally resulting in the layering of the vocal track of one song seamlessly over the music track of another.

- Digital Download : The process of transferring a digital file from one computer to another. For music, MP3 is the most popular format, although one may now have the option of buying high quality FLAC lossless files.

- Disintermediation : The elimination of intermediaries in the supply chain, which is also referred to as "Cutting The Middleman Out".

- DIY : Do It Yourself

- DRM (Digital Rights Management): DRM technologies attempt to control the use of digital media by preventing access, copying or conversion to other formats by consumers and their peers. In terms of music, DRM technologies are used in cases where the copyright owner chooses to control the ways in which content (in a recording, for instance) is used or misused. This usually is an attempt to stop illegal copying, "ripping" or file sharing.

- Fair Use : A doctrine in US copyright law allowing limited use of copyrighted material without requiring permission from copyright owners for such uses as commentary, criticism, news reporting, research, teaching or scholarship.

- FLAC : Free Loss less Audio Codec is a file format for audio data compression that does not remove information from the audio stream.

- Grand Right : The legal rights necessary to stage an opera, play with music, or a work of musical theater.

- Gratis: Without charge; FREE.

- Harry Fox Agency : The Harry Fox Agency (HFA) is an organization that represents music publishers for mechanical and digital licensing in the US. It issues licenses and collects and distributes royalties on behalf of its affiliated publishers. This includes licensing for the recording and reproduction of CDs, ringtones and Internet downloads. HFA does not issue synchronization (synch) licenses for the use of music in advertising, movies, music videos and television programs after 2002. HFA also conducts royalty examinations, investigates and negotiates new business opportunities, and pursues piracy claims.

- Copyright Registration : A record stating the creation date of a work and its content, so that in the event of infringement or plagiarism, the copyright owner can produce a copy of the work from an official source.

- Creative Commons : This term refers to both an organization and a set of licenses. The Creative Commons organization is a non-profit organization headquartered in the US devoted to   expanding the range of creative works available for others to build upon legally and to share. Creative Commons license are those licenses issued by the Creative Commons, which depending on which version is used, removes some of the restrictions of normal copyright protection (i.e. some rights reserved).

- Cross Collateral Method: A clause in recording and publishing agreements allowing the recording or publishing company to recoup outstanding advance balances from one album release with revenues from the next forthcoming release(s) and/or in the case of a multiple rights deal (i.e., a 360 deal) from various sources such as music publishing royalties, concert fees, merchandise sales, etc.

- Cue: Music used in the context of a television or film production.

- Cue Sheet : A document that itemizes music used in a television or film production by title, composer, publisher, duration and type of music usage (e.g., background, fea-ture, and theme). The cue sheet is normally prepared by the producer of the television or film production.

- DAI (Digital Audio Identification) : The use of pattern recognition, or "fingerprinting", to identify musical works aired on radio, by attempting to match them against a BDS library of known works.

- Derivative Work : Is a new work derived from one or more pre-existing works, such as a remix of a song, acoustic version, or a song based on a poem, etc. For deriva-tive works, the original copyright holders may have a claim in the new version even if they are not the creators of the derivative work.

- Black Box Income : In the music industry context, this term refers to royalty income, usually mechanical royalty income from foreign territories that has not yet been collected by the Publisher, or royalties that cannot be attributed to specific works or copyright owners. This income may come from the result of audits, adjustments or international sources.

- Blog : Blog is short for "web log" and usually refers to a website with an on-line personal journal or diary type commentary on events and opinions within a specific area of popular culture.

- Census : An analysis of ALL music used by a licensee during a specific reporting period.

- Collapsed Copyright : A term used to signify that the creator owns and controls their own copyrights in both their musical works and master sound recordings

- Composer : A creator of music and melody and composition.

- Controlled Composition : A clause in many North American recording contracts in which the recording artist – as a songwriter - agrees to a reduced mechanical royalty rate (usually 75% of the current rate), if the songs on an album are composed by the artist themselves.

- Co-Publishing Agreement :A type of publishing agreement where by two or more publishers will share in the ownership of a copy right for a specific work or body of works Typically, one publisher will have full administration rights. This type of publishing agreement often applies in cases where the composer is a recording artist or producer.

- Copyright : Exclusive rights to a work, including the sole right to publish, produce, reproduce, translate, communicate to the public by telecommunication and, in some cases, rent a work. It also includes the right to perform a work in public, and under certain conditions, to exhibit in public an artistic work.

- Aggregator: A company that collects and organizes music; normally an online music distributor (i.e. CDBaby, Tune Core, IODA, The Orchard, etc.)

- Arrangement : The preparation and adaptation of an already written musical composition for presentation in other than its original form. The detailed instructions for how instruments, sounds and voices are to be used. The arrangement dictates what is played, when it is played and how it is played (usually via written music charts or other direction).

- Arrangement (2) : A new and distinctly unique version of a Public Domain musical work (song or composition). A new arrangement of a PD work can be granted a copyright.

- Arranger : A person who writes musical arrangements

- Audit (audit clause): An audit is the process of reviewing and analyzing financial records from record labels and music publishers. Audits are undertaken on behalf of the contracted recording artist and/or composer. An audit clause is a term in an agreement or other legal document that authorizes one party to audit another.

- Author : A creator of an artistic, literary, musical or dramatic work.

- BDS (Broadcast Data Systems): A service that tracks monitored radio, television and internet airplay of songs based on number of spins and detections.

- Big Champagne : A technology-driven media measurement company.

- Bit Torrent : A peer-to-peer file sharing (P2P) communications protocol.

LIST OF MUSIC INDUSTRY TRADE ORGANIZATIONS

- National Association of Record Merchandisers (NARM).
- National Academy of Recording Arts and Sciences (NARAS).
- Recording Industry Association of America (RIAA).
- National Music Publishers Association/Harry Fox Agency (NMPA/HFA).
- National Association of Broadcasters (NAB).
- Nashville Songwriters Association International (NSAI).
- Country Music Association (CMA).
- Gospel Music Association (GMA).
- International Tape Association (ITA).
- National Association of Music Merchants (NAMM).
- Video Software Dealers Association (VSDA).

MORE TERMS

- Adaptation : A new version of a song that is inspired by an original work whether by different interpretation or instrumentation.

- Administration: The practice and process of business functions relating to a catalogue of works or individual works as well as collection and distribution of fees and royalties and all other responsibilities that relate to the use of a musical work or sound recordings.

- Agent/Agency : Music agents, otherwise known as booking agents, are the people who help make the live music happen. A good agent with well-placed connections can help get a band in front of the right audience to increase their profile. Agents work closely with promoters and record labels to get the bands on their books the proper exposure. Music agents also negotiate with promoters and venues for performance contracts and arrangements towards accommodation.

- Harry Fox Agency (for-profit branch of the NMPA)
- Indian Music Industry (IMI)
- International Federation of the Phonographic Industry (IFPI)
- Irish Recorded Music Association (IRMA)
- Latin Academy of Recording Arts & Sciences (LARAS)
- Mechanical-Copyright Protection Society (MCPS)
- Music Canada (MC)
- Musicians Benevolent Fund (MBF)
- Musicians' Union (MU)
- National Academy of Recording Arts and Sciences (NARAS)
- National Association of Recording Merchandisers (NARM)
- National Music Publishers Association (NMPA)
- Philippine Association of the Record Industry (PARI)
- PRS for Music (PRSM)
- Recording Artists' Coalition (RAC)
- Recording Industry Association of America (RIAA)
- Recording Industry Association of Japan (RIAJ)
- Recording Industry Association of New Zealand (RIANZ)
- Recording Industry of South Africa (RISA)
- Society of European Stage Authors & Composers (SESAC)
- SoundExchange (SE).
- Screen Actors Guild (SAG).
- The Songwriters Guild of America (SGA).
- The Songwriters Guild of America (SGA).

LIST OF MUSIC INDUSTRY ORGANIZATIONS & PROS

- Academy of Country Music (ACM)
- Alliance of Artists and Recording Companies (AARC)
- American Association of Independent Music (A2IM)
- American Federation of Musicians (AFM)
- American Federation of Television and Radio Artists (AFTRA)
- American Society of Composers, Authors and Publishers (ASCAP)
- American Guild of Musical Artists (AGMA).
- American Guild of Variety Artists (AGVA).
- Argentine Chamber of Phonograms and Videograms Producers (CAPIF)
- Asosiasi Industri Rekaman Indonesia (ASIRI)
- Associação Fonográfica Portuguesa (AFP)
- Associação Brasileira dos Produtores de Discos (ABPD)
- Association of Independent Music (AIM)
- Australian Recording Industry Association (ARIA)
- Billboard Magazine, known for the Billboard Hot 100
- British Phonographic Industry (BPI)
- Broadcast Music Incorporated (BMI)
- Country Music Association (CMA)
- Federation of the Italian Music Industry (FIMI)
- Gesellschaft (GEMA) in Germany
- Harry Fox Agency (for-profit branch of the NMPA)

- R and R (Radio Records) : An industry trade publication.

- Returns : Unsold records or tapes sent back to manufacturers for cash credit to buyer's account.

- Royalties : A contractual payment to an artist or producer representing a percentage of all actual record sales.

- Sampling : An electronic digital process in which an original analog sound is converted to a binary code for later playback in an electronic storage device.

- Scale : A fee assessed by unions on behalf of its members representing the minimum payment to be charged for work.

- UPC (Universal Product Code) : An identifying mark on packaging which is used by digital scanning devices for inventory control.

- Wholesale : The price manufacturers charge for a product to its distributors. This price represents the manufacturers expense in producing the product plus a profit.

- House Producer : A producer who is usually an employee of a record company.

- House Music : A style of mixing music wherein different artists and albums are combined to produce a continuous dance track.

- Independent Record Company : A record company that does not provide full manufacturing and distribution services.

- Independent Promotion Person : Freelance professional used by companies to augment its own staff.

- Independent Producer : Freelance creative production executive hired by companies on a project by project basis.

- Jukebox : A coin operated electronic record player.

- List price : The retail price of a project.

- Master : The finished production reduced to a two track tape. Subsequent copies are made in several formats for resale.

- Mechanical : A license given by a copyright owner authorizing the reproduction of records and tapes.

- Needle Drop/Laser Drop : A fee assessed by a music supplier for using their music digitally or manually as a background.

- One Stop : A sub-distributor whose clients are usually smaller record retail outlets and jukebox operators.

- P &D (Pressing and Distribution) : An arrangement between large and small companies wherein the large company will provide these service to the smaller one for a fee.

- Payola : The illegal giving or receiving of any gratuity to obtain favorable radio or television play.

- Polyvinyl Chloride : A petroleum derivative that serves as the raw material in the manufacturing of vinyl discs.

- Demographic : A statistical representation of an audience segment.

- Digital: In recording and playback the technology wherein the encoded/decoded information is represented as a binary code, series of ones and zeros.

- Doubling : A recording technique which requires a musician or singer to perform the same art twice on a different recording track.

- Electromagnetic recording : The process in which program material is magnetically encoded onto a medium usually magnetic tape.

- FCC (Federal Communications Commission) : Government agency responsible for licensing all radio, television, satellite, and telephone communications.

- FTC (Federal Trade Communication) : Government agency responsible for regulation of interstate commerce.

- F. M. (Frequency Modulation) : In radio communication a station whose carrier signal is changed by changes in source frequency.

- Free Goods : Records supplied by manufacturers at no charge as an incentive for sales.

- Freelancer : A writer or an artist who sells his services to employers without a long-term commitment to any one of them.

- Grand Rights : A license issued by a copyright holder through its performing rights organization for use of material in musical drama.

- Grammy: An award given annually by NARAS.

- Contractor : The person, required by union contracts, to hire performers. This person is paid double scale.

- Cooperative Advertising-coop : An advertising scheme wherein a record company will share advertising costs of a product with a retailer. This becomes shared advertising with mutual benefits.

- Counterfeiting : The illegal practice and process of copying a record (tape, CD) and then offering the copies for sale as originals.

- Creative Services : Department within a record company responsible for album covers, posters and other visual sales tools.

- Cross Collateral Method : A clause within recording contacts allowing the profits from each successful recording to be used to pay for the expenses of unsuccessful recordings under the same contractual arrangement.

- Crossover : A record intended for a specialized audience but finds success with other such audiences.

- Cut out : A record or tape that has reached the sales saturation in the marketplace. These items are them sold at tremendous discounts to dealers with the expectation that additional profit will be realized after the maximum of new record sales point.

- DAT (Digital Audio Tape): A high quality recording/playback technology which uses pulse-code modulation to encode information onto a tape.

- DBS (Direct Broadcast Satellite) : A method of program distribution which uses a high power satellite to transmit a signal to a highly defined coverage area.

- DeFacto Network : A broadcast scheme wherein independent broadcast stations not affiliated with a dedicated network provides access to program suppliers for limited times.

KEY MUSIC INDUSTRY TERMS

- 360 Deal: Also referred to as "multiple rights deal", 360 deals are exclusive recording artist contracts that allow a record label to receive a percentage of the earnings from ALL of a band's activities instead of just album sales.

- Advance : A fee paid to an artist as part of the royalty compensation package.

- Artist & Repertoire (A&R) : Department within record company responsible for talent acquisition.

- AM : In electronic communications, a type of radio station whose signal is encoded by its carrier wave being Amplitude Modulated.

- ANALOG : The electronic representation of a sound wave as a physical copy.

- ARB : The American Research Bureau is a television ratings company.

- Birch Report : A radio ratings service.

- Billboard : A leading trade industry magazine whose charts are used extensively.

- Bootlegging : The illegal practice of recording an artist without permission and then offering the recording for sale.

- CD (Compact Disc) : A format for recordings using electronic digital technology.

- Chart : Trade newspaper listing of records according to their relative popularity. Charts are an important barometer of a record's success.

- PHANTOM LABEL: This term identifies with a false record company that represents one individual who is solely out to control an artist. This is usually ran by bad representation who forge fraudulent deals to keep their clients bound to them.

- ROAD WORK: This term represents the work that one must complete to make sure all angles of their administrative duties are taking care of such as, copyrights, publishing agreements, licenses etc.

- SPARE TIRE: This term identifies with having a backup talent to mold your musical repertoire. This often relates to being a triple threat and can be very beneficial for the artist.

- THE ZONE: A level or state of perfection within a creative session or performance, that push the artist to perform beyond their normal strengths.

- VIBE KILLERS: This term identifies with individuals who are out to distract, cause conflict and ruin the creative session of musicians, artists, producers etc.

PAVED TERMS

- ACCIDENTS: Incidents that aim to destroy, damage or halt your career such as lawsuits, contract disputes and or label disagreements etc.

- CARPOOL: This term identifies with the team that you allow to improve and rep-resent your brand as well as your career.

- CURRENT TIME: This term represents the grid of time that the Major Record La-bels operate on.

- DEAD END: This term represents a point and place in your career that you can't go beyond. This usually happens when following trends or losing sight of your visual direction for your career.

- DETOUR: This term represents a time in your career when you have to make a sudden shift or change.

- DITCH: This term represents a point in your career where you can't seem to get ahead or out of certain career ruts.

- HEAVY TRAFFIC: This term identifies with the hundreds of thousands, if not millions who happen to be in your field as well as going after the same goals. With an overwhelming amount of people rushing to be known, it cause for the career lane that you travel to become backed up.

- HITCH HIKERS: This term identifies with certain individuals who tag along on your journey as freeloaders, opportunists etc., who are out to only gain and not to give.

- HYBRID PRODUCERS: This term identifies with new age producers who are innovating new ways to create music, without the control of major labels.

quarters and deadlines in which they were set. This will be your guide to navigating towards your goals completion within your music career.

Cementing this concept for PAVED allowed for my knowledge to be identified with the struggle of so many individuals. We all want to get to where we have to go in our career with accurate time and precision, it would be very helpful if we had a guide as such. I wanted this book to be the stepping stone for future innovators who are looking to help individuals reach there goals accurately through technology. This book was designed with a clear understanding factor of innovation. I gained a lot from writing this book and I know the masses will as well. This knowledge will help you acquire success on your journey through this business, embrace it and you will accomplish everything that you need accomplished.

"I wish you all the best on your journeys and I will see you within the light of Success...-Silkk "The Shocker" Miller

The PAVED Concept

The concept for PAVED is geared towards the technological sense of traveling and the over-trending use of GPS devices that people use daily towards reaching accurate locations as well as destinations in a quick time. Starting out in this business, many lack that knowledge of having a sense of where they want to go in their careers. It's evident that the modern world relies solely on accuracy through the use of technology. This at times becomes the substitute for our own good judgement of accurate memory to that of a GPS device. As I continued on with with my motive I'd began to wonder, "What if this futuristic focal point could work for those pursuing their dreams? Who said there couldn't be a GPS device so powerful that its sole purpose was to help us for our future?". In reality, that device hasn't been delivered to this time period yet...but maybe this book could serve as a blueprint to those possible devices of the near future.

Our sense of direction as well as self-reliance will be reestablished, redefining balance with our technological counterpart. It's been proven in studies that in this day and age, we travel along the highways and byways of life relying on GPS devices to choose the best possible solution of a route or path that will get us to "WHERE EVER", promptly. This device even will ask you if you'll be traveling by walking, car or bus etc., while accurately granting you an estimated frame of time of when each reliable source of transportation would arrive at your destination. I continue to research these devices then I was hit again, "What if this approach could be geared towards understanding the essentials of the Music Industry in a map form?".

This book's approach could very well serve as that map, blueprint and that new standard route to embark upon for accurate success. This dynamic approach will give stability and structure for a multitude of aspiring music professionals. Though there are many outdated methodical books that are being circulated to a wide range of individuals, the teachings and approaches aren't sticking or grasping the attentions of today's aspiring music professionals. I aimed to create that up to date method as well as must have literature for musical success within the modern world. In this business timing is everything and so is our goals. This is why we set them in high demand to be accomplished and completed precisely on the dates,

PREFACE

THE REASON FOR PAVED

After being overwhelmed with so many questions about this business and not having the time to answer them all, I decided to create this book. I took the time to decipher the riddled knowledge of this industry to present this guide to you. Even while I was doing the research to bring the knowledge of those many questions that aspiring music professionals ask, I'd begun to see this industry much clearer than ever before. The music industry is a puzzle inside an even bigger puzzle. Cracking its codes and placing the correct pieces in order can become very over-whelming. The journey led me to the realization that the majority of the information that's out there about the music industry is combined with accurate and inaccurate information. I was placed in a bewilderment, asking myself "Where is the solid information of this business?" , The thing that made it even more of an intricate puzzle was the fact that the inaccurate information, is what's being pushed, recycled and distributed to the people. My first thought was that it would take too long to create this book but I instantly became very determined to complete it after researching so much false information. I knew from my experience that I had the knowledge that people needed. It was my job to give it to them. Though there were many who said I shouldn't lose any sleep over this, I knew that I needed to do this book. I had to do this for the millions of aspiring individuals who want to make name for themselves in this business and didn't have a lot of time to do it. By creating this guide I would limit the mistakes that's often made by the masses in this business. With a zeal of sophistication and less complication to succeed. I needed to create something that would be identifiable with anyone in music as well as give clarity and understanding about some essential tools you need to have. In this world we're all searching for an easier or more efficient solution to elevate our careers, in a timely fashion. So as I continued to brainstorm with an array of formulas and ideas it hit me, a GPS that can get you to where you need to go accurately within your career.

NOTES

Success isn't the amount of money you have nor make but its conquering your goals with accomplish able motives, creating avenues of multiple streams of wealth. There is an old saying that many follow to this day that says "If you give a man a fish he'll eat for a day but if you teach that same man how to fish, he will eat for a lifetime". This is a standard passage that many moguls live by to reproduce their wealth. Embedding motivational tools into your mind will push you to go beyond any level that has been placed to test you on your journey. Though many will say that pushing hard work defines a standard cliche but it is the truest action that will give you the best leverage for your career.

The principle agenda you should have for your career is to set goals for yourself. Plan out your approach and aim to accomplish them no matter how long or how hard the journey becomes. This is your time to live out your dreams. No regrets or doubts should seep into your mind. Wealth is yours and you can and will succeed in this business. Be the best you that you've ever been. Doing all of this will define longevity for your career and your wealth. Enjoy this moment, you've worked hard to get here. Never let someone tell you that you don't deserve success because you do.

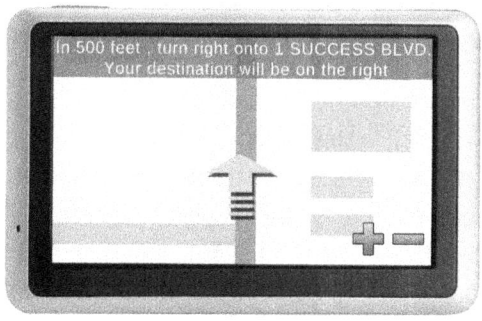

Chapter 12:
YOU HAVE ARRIVED!!!

Now that you've finally reached your destination, you have properly gained the essential knowledge of this industry. Even though throughout your career you will travel down many roads, take plenty of routes towards newer journeys, set new goals and capitalize on or reestablish your success. The experience that you've acquired will be there to guide you through. As you begin to incorporate this knowledge into your arsenal, try thinking of it as your newer sense of direction. A sense of direction is considered to be the most precious gift you can have while navigating your way thru this riddled business. Even with a GPS you can still lose your way.

Success is only the first milestone you can achieve in this business. The ultimate achievement is succeeding in this industry. When you can say that you succeeded amongst some of the most prestigious and elite that this industry has birthed, is when you have reached a plateau that only a few have been blessed to surpass. Dreaming and thinking bigger than you've ever thought allows for you to push through the thresholds that may aim to prevent you from soaring. Capitalize on your character, embrace the gifts that makes you a unique and bold force within this business. Never fear your passion or the journey and roads that it will lead you down. You have the drive to conquer any setback or flaw within the business. Believe in your craft because it will not let you down.

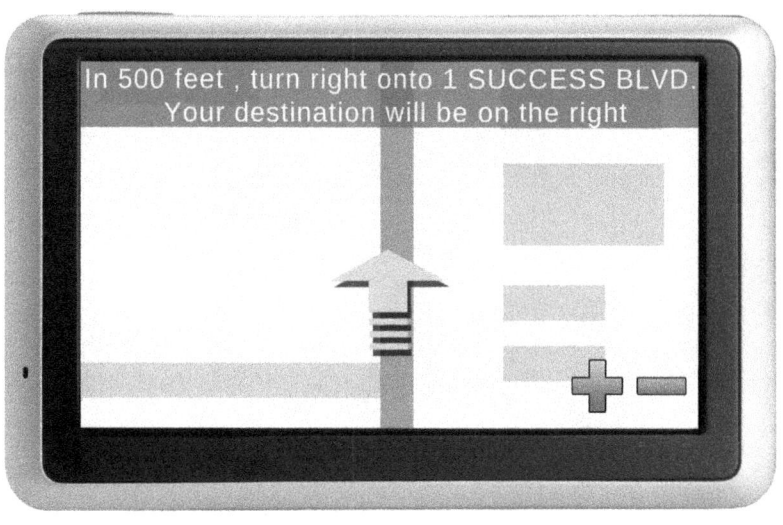

NOTES

- Creative Branding: As a brand you have the tools as well as team to create some monumental things. Try using this advantage in creating more streams of revenue out-side of music.

- Charity Work: When you give with no alternate motive you will eventually gain back more than you've given out.

- Wise Spending: Just because the wealth is in your possession doesn't mean that you have to spend frivolously. Be wise about what your spending.

- Pay Your Taxes: When you're at the height of your success and wealth is flowing in abundantly, you may tend to lose track of filing your taxes. Keep in mind that this should be the very first thing on your to do list, NEVER play around with the IRS

- Smart Banking Practices: Saving your money would be very wise, keep in mind that you should choose a banking institution that will have your best interest when it comes to your assets.

- Capitalize Your Earnings: Everything that you earn within this business you have the power to increase as well as capitalize on it. This practice also helps with saving and managing your funds.

Always remember to be watchful who is around you or who's aiming to get a slice of your wealth pie. In this industry, some people make careers out of getting other people's money, always stay alert and watchful of who you befriend and you'll will remain wealthy.

"PAY or PLAY" Clause

The "Pay or Play" Clause is an option that the record company offers to artists regarding their project. The company will offer to pay you an amount of money that is equal to the minimum union scale amount that is used to complete an album or choose to just play your record without the intent of distributing it or promoting it. In the case of them choosing to pay you off, make sure that your contract has ended or that they decide to terminate it. If you fail to take care of business this will be the easiest way for the Majors to keep you on hold, in return ruining your career and capital growth.

KEEPING YOUR WEALTH

With all there is to gain within this industry, there may come a time when you'll lose a lot more than you would intake. Even though it can be a bumpy ride when it comes to earning capital within your career you will obtain wealth, to keep it proves to be the most difficult part. Many believe that when you've obtained wealth, you can multiply it and they are right. With the proper investing practices and work ethic this will be possible. I would advise you to always pay any taxes, fees or other monies that may be due to multiple constituents, this is for your own protection as well as freedom.

As we look into the word Wealth we can learn that it represents an abundance of valuable possessions or money. This affluence is what drives you to pursue success as well as prosperity in all that you do. We've all ended up on that road to riches, in search of fortunate means or a substance for purity. That road has never been easy nor will it ever become but in essence you will become wealthy.

Here is a List of Tips on Keeping Your Wealth;

- Wise Investing: When you are given wealth, try to invest a percentage into active products or companies that with increase your share.

money and it is rightfully owed to you.

ALL IN

Outside from receiving royalties from a project you also will have to give or pay a percentage to other constituents as well. This brings us to the All In service fee that is subtracted from your royalties to pay for producer fees , engineering fees etc., that played a major part in your projects success. The Majors will initially document this into the contract and you will be obligated to pay the percentage amount that was agreed upon even if the project does well or not. This is commonly worded into the contract as Funds , monies given or distributed to the talent to pay for extra fees. Once you paid out the fees you will be able to retain the rest of your money but could very well end up with none if a certain criteria isn't met.

Understanding Formulas

When it comes down to asking for the correct amount of money within this industry, if you know how to negotiate well, the Majors will agree to establishing a Formula for your advances. This clause represents the motive to improve or increase the percentages of your album's deal as your career reaches a successful point . Keep in mind that this clause is a time sensitive agreement in which earnings have to be met within 6-18 months after the project has been released. This is a way for the Majors not to increase the formula once sales have increased beyond the allotted time frame. Many times to ensure that accurate funds will still be given out a floor amount will be established, meaning the company can't give you anything lower than what you've agreed upon. Once this is cemented within the contract the company will comply with the funding do to a ceiling amount they create and this will place a cap over any monies the Majors will not go beyond. So it would be wise to try to bid on an amount that will make since for your financial future.

Advances to Recoupment

This is where it tends to get a bit tricky for most individuals who are newly signed to a label, because so many fall of or lose monies all because of mismanagement. Advances are the initial compensation that is given to an Artist once they've signed to a label. Depending on the status of the talent, an Advance can range from the hundreds of thousands to the millions. Where a lot of people lose their way with these monies is the thought that its non repayable. Take note that every penny has to be repaid from any advance. The Record Label will give you an advance mainly towards project related things such as studio time, touring, musicians, travel expenses etc. Yet some will spend the money on various non-music related things such as cars, houses and many other luxuries. Like I stated earlier, you have to remain smart about your investments in this business.

Once the Majors grants you an advance they will also hold that amount against future income on royalties, albums , deals etc., until the monies is recouped. This is what they refer to as a Recoupment. Always think twice before you begin spending your advance money because it really is considered to be a loan. Keep in mind that it is considered to be a Cross Collateralized method once the Majors decide to hold royalties on future albums because of an advance not being recouped from the first project's royalties.

Escalations

Escalations represents an increase of royalty percentages from over achieved album sales and or future advances that is owed to individuals who have contributed to the success of a project. These types of payments in contrast to points are very difficult to receive, due to the Majors not really wanting to grant you anything higher than what was agreed. Take note that you will have to stay on top of this matter to receive these monies, so in other words you have to force the Majors hand a bit. Remember its your money and it is rightfully owed to you.

bilingual and or understand your business terms you need to always have your team of professional representatives look over your contracts and business agreements because if not, signing a contract of such could leave you in a very bad position or ditch within your career.

On top of the Majors handing out gratis material on your behalf, they will also give away Promo copies of the material to various promotional outlets such as licensors, radio stations, film companies etc., and specifically coining them as a not for sale item. These exclusive copies are often used to build the fan base of a specific talent as well as showcase what the company is representing. Its very seldom that the Majors would distribute these copies of a talent that they do not plan on investing in. Like I said before the talent is the product in this business and that's how the Majors capitalize on that fact.

Return Privileges and Reserves

The Music Industry of today offers music retailers a 100% Return Privilege on all material that does not sale, guaranteeing the retailers full compensation. This clause was established on the basis of the retailers purchasing large quantities of CD's to sell from within their establishment. Retailers would have to at least aim to sell the product in order to be granted a full refund. If they fail to comply with that clause penalties are often issued by the record companies that they initially made the purchase with. The penalty could range from 15%-25% of excess records that are returned. Often times this practice can damage your initial record sales, especially since your material can be returned at a 100% value of it was purchased for. Even the Majors will put a hold on your royalties based off of them protecting their interests and assets. This will put you in the negative until your project starts flying off of the shelves of the retailers stores. This is a practice that the Majors like to refer to as Reserves of Interest, which occurs when the label is in fear of losing money from your project, entitling them to place a hold on all monies owed to you until they begin to see sale progress. This only works toward hard physical copies of your material such as CD's, so this means digital material will be in the clear of this clause because their is no stock nor inventory on the material. Keep in mind that the Majors will try to slip this within the contract, be very watchful and always have your representatives check for this.

For starters, a point is equivalent to being 1% and is often used as or considered to be Album points that pertain directly to the percentages awarded from a project's retail price and or basic dealer price of its CD or digital download. These points are normally divided in various ways such as, points for the entire project; points for particular recordings or contributions on the project or just points on the initial gross/net sales of the project. It would be wise to note that not all individuals will be awarded points for a project and could very well opt out of future points if a certain Label can't agree upon a valid deal for the points . Most times in the business, the Majors will structure a point deal based on the contingency of how efficient record sales are doing. For instance, if a producer is given a deal where they're entitled to 3 points for the project and escalations off of proceeds, if the record or project does well the producer's initial starting points will increase in value every time the project reaches a certain sale goal or surpasses certain project thresholds. This contingency is often only granted to high end talent but could very well be negotiated within the contract. Always have every clause or any quotes of extra details in writing for your peace of mind.

FREE GOODS (Gratis) & Promos

In chapter 7 we spoke about the various types of royalties that can be earned within the business. We also learned that these royalties are generated from license/leasing agreements for the usage of music to record sales but take note that record companies can distribute Gratis (Latin for Free) copies of your material known as Free Goods, exempting those works from receiving or qualifying for royalties. This incentive is for retailers to distribute more quantities of the material. So at times the Majors will give an additional 10-15% more to be distributed along with the retailers initial order. The record company is not compensated while doing this but in return they will not grant royalties on the extra items they shipped out and your total amount of royalty compensation will take a hit. This at times causes a chink in the chain of the business relationship between the label and their talent because of this free clause. In this Industry, sometimes Majors will present contracts and agreements to their talent that will simply state that all royalties or monies that is to be compensated or awarded on certain projects will be Gratis, meaning you will get nothing. Unless you're

Chapter 11: CAPITAL

Understanding How Contracts Work

In this chapter we'll be breaking down some key points on how capital works within the Music Industry. Please take note that your capital wealth will only multiply if you push to evolve your entire repertoire. In this business wealth is obtainable with hard work and the wisdom of knowing how to manage large sums of monies that will be awarded to you throughout your career. It will also come down to contracts and agreements of certain types of deals that will eventually cement your income. Please be advised that after you have received your residuals you shouldn't aim to spend it all at once. Doing this could very well leave you without wealth for your future. As I stated earlier, you have to be smart within this industry.

The Point System

In chapter 9, I briefly spoke about points and how companies now see them as a complete representational breakdown of how royalty percentages will be awarded or split between individuals and the company.

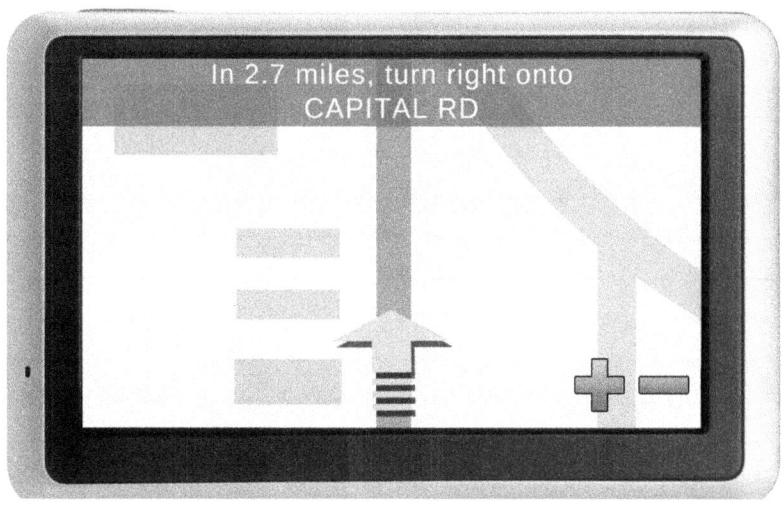

NOTES

FALLING STAR

A Falling STAR is someone who has simply fallen off and loses the popularity of their Star Quality amongst popular culture as well as the industry. Many individuals who experience this level of hardship within their careers will sometimes become attention seekers, addicted to substances, become depressed, show signs of irrational behavior in public or through the media, become hit with legal charges, create bad press and some have even died. Over the last several decades as well as in today's popular society, we've bared witness to the rise as well as fall of a large number of STARS within the entertainment realm. Even now as your reading this, I'm pretty sure some celebrity is in the news for allegations or is a trending topic on social media for their woes and troubles. Like I stated several times throughout the book, this industry isn't built for the weak, so you have to stay mentally strong or you could loss it all. The only thing that can prevent your career from ending up in a ditch is your level of focus. Remaining focused on the positive aspects of your journey and not the distractions and pit falls of fame, can elevate your mind to execute the right choices for your long term success. It takes the zeal of patience and integrity to remain an elite within this industry. Don't lose sight of your focus as well as individuality over social status.

lose sight of their initial objective for reaching success but for myself, I persevered by staying true to my craft and the goals that was at hand. You have to stay focused on your long term goals for success at all times.

Below is a breakdown of STAR levels as well as a tip about not becoming a Falling STAR;

- *STAR*: Those who reach and achieve this level of success have worked diligently on there craft and are now being recognized for their contributions nationally.

  Common Label Advance: $200,000 - $800,000

  Royalty Percentage: 15%-20%

- ***SUPERSTAR***: This level of social status is obtained by STARS who have capitalized on the expansion of their brand's creativity as well as career on a commercially successful scale. Acquiring this status grants you the complete control of any direction you'd want to take your career in.

  Common Label Advance: $500,000 - 2,000,000

  Royalty Percentage: 20%-30%

- *****MEGASTAR*****: As it comes to reaching this plateau in your career keep in mind that it is a privilege. Seldom do many achieve this level in their career or even in this business. In order to achieve such a level within your career you have to go above in beyond with your craft, exceeding well beyond the national plateau of your career leading to a following on a Global scale. If successful this will be one of the greatest accomplishments of your career.

  Common Label Advance: $1,000,000 and Up

  Royalty Percentage: 50% or more

When traveling this route you must proceed with caution. It takes a tremendous amount of courage to be a STAR in this business and beyond. Especially if you are blessed enough to reach the ranks of SUPERSTAR or even MEGASTAR. Achieving such levels of Super stardom can prove to be a positive advancement in retaining your wealth as well as success for your career. Please keep in mind that these levels can also make you lose yourself if not fully focused on your craft. This ultimately will lead to you being considered a Falling STAR, which will make it very difficult to sustain a successful or profitable career.

In the business of today, the Majors will capitalize on Super stardom and at times can shallowly make it the most important factor of your success. Record Labels will bank on the fact that social status is the ultimate way to entice followers to buy into a brand. It's an obvious fact that people will show up to support their favorite celebrity or idol based on their popularity in the business. This creates a leverage for the label's success but socially it comes down to the fact of people wanting to be apart of the "Star Experience". For example; When I started out on my journey, my main focus wasn't to become a STAR but I did. I instantly incorporated this new level of status to my advantage with a clear understanding that I'd be granted the opportunities that regular individuals wouldn't be granted. Reaching newer plateaus would put me more in demand with my fan base and the industry as well. The Majors would constantly seek me out, the paparazzi would follow and invade my privacy more, but I learned very early in my career that blindly living within such a status isn't the right choice. Sometimes superstardom can very well name its on price over your career and even your life. I've been in the presence of a multitude of Artists etc., who've soared amongst the stars yet fall while their career is still launching. A great amount of individuals who pursue a career within the business will instantly

Once you lose sight of your focus it becomes easy to merge into doing what everyone else is doing. Always keep your mind waves clear to influence your sound and style. You have to remember that you are defining who YOU are and if your big enough, EVERYONE else. For instance, establishing reachable as well as realistic goals can help you to stay driven and refreshed creatively. Although this business may try to cause you to steer off-road, the key to surviving is by knowing where your creative coverage stands. This will strengthen your mind as well as prepare you if storms are to come your way. This business isn't for the weak and you have to be stronger than the average person to effectively be considered a Trendsetter. Though many will decide to follow a trend out of obligation, keep in mind that following that path will only lead to a Dead-End for your career.

Let's analyze this term as it relates to your career;

- DEAD-END: When it comes to the industry of music, there are countless ways to find yourself at a Dead-End but the main way is to follow a trend. As an aspiring professional you wouldn't want to indulge within a trend but set the trend. This industry happens to be run by trendsetters. You have to become your own trendsetter to stand the tests of time. Many will choose to follow a trend with the thought of it being more manageable or less stressful but being yourself isn't as hard as some make it out to be. The trend will eventually run its course, while the Trendsetter will evolve and create a new trend. It's much easier to be yourself opposed to being like or following someone else. Even though following a trend will earn the Majors a quick buck or two, traveling down your own trending lane will grant you longevity in this industry. Keep in mind that you can't acquire success in this industry without your own identity.

A STAR IS BORN

The one thing that captures the attention of a large amount of people is having the opportunity and outlet to become a huge success or STAR . The thought alone alternates the lives of millions who are dreaming, aiming for that day when their light will shine from above the heavens onto the world. Though the allure of what is envisioned seems to be a picture perfect reality, you can very well endure turmoil once you've reached a higher plateau of social status.

Although you don't have to be in the music industry to be considered a STAR, this industry happens to be the home to a large percentage of STARS. This factor alone threatens the poise of many aspiring music professionals who are aiming for Super stardom. The stakes are extremely high in the business, especially since the Majors want you to mimic or imitate current trends, sounds and personas of those who already reached that plateau in order to get a break. Though it will seem as if you're at constant odds with the industry or have to constantly recreate your style, creative approach and core audience to remain relevant, don't burn your engine out just yet because you possess the power to control your Star Quality as a Trendsetter.

Below are 5 Self-Evaluation Questions that every Aspiring Music Professional should ask themselves when pursuing Super stardom in Music;

1. What type of creative force can I be in Music?

2. What are My musical goals for success as a professional?

3. What attributes do I possess within my repertoire magnifies my Star Quality?

4. Am I a Trendsetter?

5. What can I offer to this Industry that will make me an Innovator as well as Pioneer?

TRENDSETTING

In the world of music, innovational trendsetting can seem like something out of the past... literally. The pioneering aspect of creative discovery is quite limited, since the majority of the innovative process in popular culture has already been done or mastered throughout the years. Today we've bared witness to a ton of recycling, sampling and rediscovering of those golden gems of the past. Finding yourself within an innovative space while trendsetting in your career takes time as well as dedication. As an aspiring individual it is solely your job to remain humble and patient in all

Chapter 10: STAR QUALITY

Understanding How Contracts Work

The Music Industry is filled with a multitude of creative personalities and at times the corporate umbrella can be accredited for creating certain gimmicks behind those personalities. However, when it comes to being defined as a STAR or having what many professionals call Star Quality, you have to already possess the gene or gift within you. Many are born with this attribute and usually will capitalize on its strengths when working on their niche. While some attain or work on gaining this strength from observing their idols, heros or train themselves ferociously to acquire it. These individuals represent a different dynamic to the expression being talented, proving that you must work twice as hard to maintain your quality. In popular culture the terms STAR, SUPERSTAR or even MEGASTAR are used to identify with the statuses of certain celebrities within the music business who has achieved a certain level or plateau in social status.

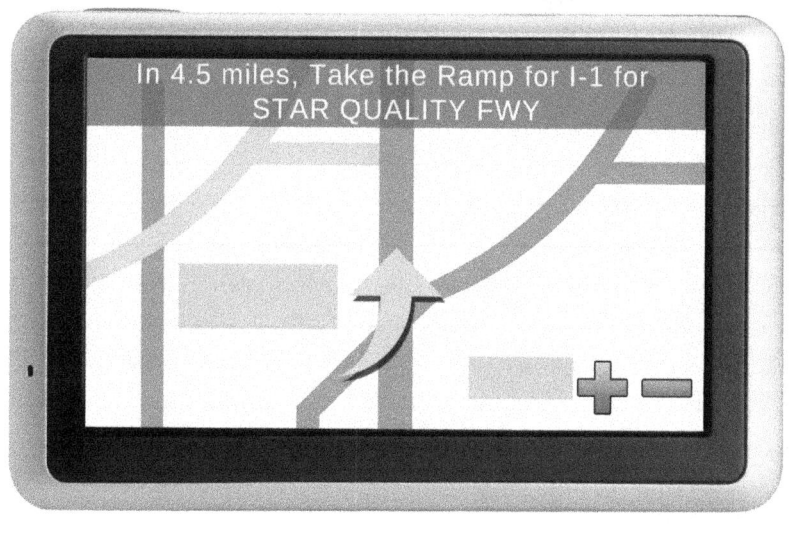

NOTES

Below is a list of common reasons that will lead to a termination of an agreement or contract:

1. Music Goes out of Print or Shelved

2. Licensing Agreement Expires

3. Distribution Becomes Halted

4. Legal Issues

5. Label Goes Bankrupt or Takes a Buy Out

6. Breach of Contract

7. Artistic Difference

8. Managerial Disagreements

9. Poor Record Sales

10. Poor Deal

11. Ownership Disputes

Though there are thousands of ways that lead to a termination, just make sure you have all of your angles covered if faced with this situation. Always keep your team of legal reps informed at all time in these types of scenarios. It will be a very wise approach on your behalf.

Take note to always leave egos outside of the session and everything will come out successful.

Take a Deal or Not

Once you've reached a comfortable place within your career you'll begin to ask yourself "Should I take a Deal?" and any conclusion that you come to should symbolize growth for your success. Some will say that you don't need a label of any sort to become successful but as I stated earlier, you have to work very hard and the Indie route isn't for everybody. Even though CD's aren't in high demand since the coming age of digital music, you can still make a profit for your work in that form. In the past, many pursued the Majors primarily for financial advancement and in return found themselves in worst positions due to bad dealing or blindly accepting responsibilities that they couldn't handle. With or without a deal you can acquire success and stability if you put in the work. You have to set the bar and overcome it no matter what, the choice is yours.

Terminating the Agreement

Terminating a Deal or an Agreement can be a very stressful process to endure. If you ever have to endure this in your career try to remain humble as well as very professional. You will learn that handling business the right way earns you a lot of respect in this industry and increases your opportunity potential. Many factors will lead individuals to parting ways with a company or label in their career. Keep in mind that these types of transitions can either enhance your success or diminish your success but in the end you have to work out the best route possible for your stability. The business relationship between the Majors and the talent they form agreements with has become very cold over the last few decades . There used to be a time when the company you signed with would mold you into the best talent possible but somehow those days were very short lived and may never return. As stated earlier, Major labels are ran by corporations who view their stable of talent as products. That view alone causes a rift in the relationship and will ultimately lead to contracts or agreements being terminated. The prudent approach that the Majors have towards the Artist's material or work ethic causes many professionals to become frustrated in their craft. Take note you should never allow anyone to frustrate your craft.

Here's what your Split Sheet should consist of;

1. Names of Collaborators (as it will appear on credits)
2. Mailing Address of Collaborators (to receive a copy)
3. Roles of Constituents (Writer, Producer, Musician etc.)
4. Percentages of Individual Contributions
5. Percentage Split of Producer's 100% pie share (usually 50/50 if multiple producers)
6. Percentage Split of Writers 100% pie share (usually evenly split)
7. Performance Rights Organizations (if any)
8. Publishing Company (if any)
9. Birthdate & Signatures of All Contributors
10. Social Security Number or EIN (Tax I.D) of All Parties
11. Miscellaneous Information
12. Sign & Date

• Create Freely: When you begin to collaborate you will notice immediately if egos are high or if some individuals want to control the entire collaboration. Keep in mind that this will not be a very good collaboration if all parties can't equally and freely participate.

• Be Yourself: While collaborating never stop being who you are, its the most important attribute to add to the vibe

• REMOVE ALL VIBE KILLERS!!!! There is nothing more important than getting rid of all distractions that will potentially kill your vibe in a collaborative session. These distractions are normally consisting of entourages, overly boastful and arrogant talent, negative commentary, closed minded collaborators etc.

you have to embrace and feel the collaboration because it enhances the creative experience, taking your talent into another level or THE ZONE of the session. This attribute represents an almost perfect or euphoric vibe that gives the senses within your talents an extra boost of energy, adrenaline and creativity. For instance, you may hear some singers say that once they enter into The Zone, they can hit higher pitches or can completely perform with accuracy without blemish or flaw. Throughout you career you'll eventually have several moments as such but make sure the chemistry of the collaboration is sincere and non-restricted.

Here are some tips on having a successful collaboration and how not to kill the vibe of the session or the people your collaborating with;

• SPLIT SHEET: The first thing to establish before and after entering into a collaborative session is a valid Split Sheet, an essential binding agreement that collaborators establish to put in place fair percentages of royalties generated from publishing. Though it isn't a legal requirement, having this agreement in place serves as the most effective and safe way to avoid drama when it comes down to shares. Take note that this tool helps with tracking down all parties involved with the collaboration, documenting their initial contributions. Along with creating the Split Sheet it would be a wise approach to document your intentions as well as the role you played or will be playing in the project or session. This will save you the headache of misunderstandings or disputes about everyone's place and contribution when the time comes to receive royalties and residuals for the work. There are many different approaches to creating an effective Split Sheet but creating a standard form can will do you just fine.

The latest innovative computer technology for music has become very high in demand over the past decade or so, pushing suppliers of these products to create a mass amount for consumers to indulge in. With these innovations in place it has become virtually easier to make compositions in the comfort of your own home, without the monitoring or control of a corporate conglomerate . This factor alone has catapulted a sudden growth spurt of up and coming independent producers infamously known throughout the business as Beat Makers, who collectively create full productions within home based studios using tools such as lap tops, musical work-stations/instruments, beat machines and digital recording software. These innovative creations has allowed for this newer generation of "Hybrid Producers" to become very successful by digitally leasing or selling their completed tracks to Artists, Songwriters and Record Labels . These producers normally start out as independent free-lancers whose operations consist primarily of creating and submitting their works to underground talent, generating a respectable local buzz. Once their catalogue of music grows or their following transcends outside of their local territory, most will sign with publishers, managers, agents or production companies to get placement opportunities on a major scale. Take note that even if this isn't apart of your musical repertoire, incorporating this can prove to be a very successful addition for your career in the future but keep in mind that taking this path can lead you to enduring heavy traffic.

The art of collaboration is a very intricate skill to develop as well as master in this business. Like many other skills, collaboration takes time, nurturing as well as the right chemistry to achieve its perfection. Often times taking place within studio sessions or an array of different creative places, many professionals will concur that having the proper balance to create, produce and work with others gives you that in-demand factor while collaborating. For example, When we look at the formula that's being used towards features and guest appearances from Artists or that most sought Producer to work with, we instantly recognize the chemistry that they possess while collaborating. Though there are some great collaborations as well as collaborators out there, not all of what is being played, streamed or promoted is a great collaboration. What makes a great collaboration isn't the "Big Name Stars" that you put together but the chemistry of that project and the legacy it leaves. A large multitude of artistic individuals will say that

How a Production Deal Works

Opposed to seeking a recording deal to jump start their careers, many individuals such as Artists, Songwriters etc., link up with producers to pursue or go after Production Deals to gain a good vantage point within the Majors. In most cases these types of deals start off as an alternative to having representation. Whereas the Production Company or Producer would legally act as your representative and would have the power to package, present and or place your material into the hands of the Majors. Signing a deal like this usually plays out in the favor of the Producer/Production Company as well as the Record Label they've formed the agreement with. This is usually due to blindly signing under the Production Company. The Majors will typically go into Joint Labeling (Collaborative Projects) or third-party partnerships with Production Companies on the contingency of working exclusively with the talent that may be signed under the label or signed under the Production Company/Producer. This pact also indicates that the Majors would be involved with the Production Company/Producer or their Artist for a one time project or a per project basis, while gradually becoming involved with promotional and distributive services, assembling project teams and or financial backing.

In the event of these types of arrangements the Majors will demand Artists to sign an Inducement Letter (Side Letter) to ensure and cement their responsibility of personally delivering a completed album in the case of the corporation not being able to push, market or deliver the material to the record company. With this letter in place you have to uphold the obligations of the agreement for the sake of the completed CD being aligned or tendered to the company, failing to comply will result in a breach of contract and may cause a-lot of legal troubles and damages. Keep in mind that your success doesn't have to come from this type of agreement and if you play your cards right you will end up in greater situations.

The Majors will normally break down their percentages using the point system. This typically falls on the line of a per album type of basis if you've signed a deal. For instance, let's say an Artist is given 10 points to begin with or if they're lucky 15 (in my opinion 15-20 points is fair for new artists). The label will acquire about 85-90 points for a project and will also recoup from all expenses you earn but in return grant you the option to acquire 5 additional points per album on top of the points you initially started with. This normally doesn't happen with most 360 deals because the Majors are not looking for or even betting on the success of your next potential album. If they were you wouldn't need a 360 deal. Even though they'll ease up on pressuring you to complete your project or grant you more control, don't be fooled by the leeway that they're giving because they will make their money regardless of if your project is doing well or not. Keep in mind that you have to remain wise and watchful of the deals that you agree upon. You don't want to potentially damage your career from the result of taking a bad deal.

Active and Passive Interest of 360 Deals

360 deals usually practice a form of Passive Interest. This will prevent the Majors from having any control over any dealings that you pursue. The company however, will still be entitled to royalties from your pockets that was initially agreed upon. For instance, you may sign with multiple publishers, work with whom ever you desire etc., as long as you compensate the company. But there is a clause that will also entitle the Majors to more control which is Active Interest. The Majors will slip this into the agreement, controlling who you work with, who you publish with, the company that distributes your merchandise etc. Keep in mind that these clauses within the deal proves to be ultimately within the favor of the Majors.

360 Multiple Rights Deal

Throughout your career you will come across many types of deals, contracts and agreements that may either make or break your career. The potential to succeed in this business is very high since The Majors have been in some turmoil over the last decade. The chaos started with the overwhelming growth of technological advancements for music through the use of the internet, causing the infrastructures of both Major and indie labels to change. As these innovations continue to move full speed ahead in the business, the piracy of digital music over the internet soars as well. Commonly, this type of piracy happens via digital downloading, file sharing and stream conversions of Mp3 files off of media sites. During these drastic times labels have tried to comply or compromise with the ever so changing digital pace of music but in return require an overbearing amount of profitability to be returned to their company. This leads us to discuss the age of the 360 Deal (Multiple Rights Deal) in the Music Industry, which is a legal pact that gives record companies the right to acquire greater percentages of royalties and monies from their artist's proceeds.

A 360 Deal can either work for your career or against your career's success depending on your approach. Keep in mind that these deals are normally geared towards the label or company's favor. The record companies fear that if they don't acquire this deal from their artists that they'll end up losing, failing or going bankrupt from pushing the product. So for them this is considered to be their "Win/Win" situation. They are granted a recoupment of all advances and percentages of everything that you produce such as touring, merchandising, endorsement deals, fan club rates and fees, public appearances, collaborative works such as movies, sound tracks, TV shows etc. Not to mention the royalties they'll acquire from the music you make and sale. Many view this type of deal as a legal way for a record company to swindle more money from you but in some rare cases an Artist can benefit from it. Some labels will grant those who are more established higher percentages of CD profits and/or more monies toward their advance and even after they've received additional royalties from all monies being recouped from the proceeds, may offer or give an even share of the wealth. Please take into consideration that this is an extremely rare case within the 360 agreement.

If you happen to be an established performer within this business, you'll have more say so in your contractual agreement and just might be able to maneuver around the Major's trying to get a bigger payout from your material. In this industry you have to speak up and fight for a fair contract because if you don't, you could end up with a very bad deal or a very low percentage of the profits. The Music Industry is filled with examples of individuals who were sucked dry by the Majors while being at the top of their careers and their downfalls were due to bad deals, contracts issues, destructive lifestyles, copyright/publishing issues etc. Having the power to renegotiate your deals gives you the opportunity to acquire greater profits and cement your profitability if you happen to be signed with the Majors.

It is very important to learn how to negotiate before you are even amongst the Majors because it will definitely grant you an advantage. For example; I understood how the business worked before I entered into it, so when it came down to presenting myself to the Majors I knew exactly how to negotiate a fair deal. The business side of things were novice to work through for myself, along with my brother and our team because we had the ball in our court when it came down to percentages and our overall deal. The deal we had was completely fair in my opinion because we negotiated our contract well. We didn't need much help from the Majors and we even started without an advance of compensation, that in return guaranteed us 85% of all proceeds/ royalties with the company only acquiring 15%. We also remained the sole copyright holders of our Masters (The master copy of music) which many artist's don't get to have, since the Majors specifically file separate copyrights for the material that their artist's create. This in return grants them ownership of all of their artist's master recordings. We were granted that deal by speaking up and declaring that we weren't going to be taken advantage of with our music. The type of deal we were given was considerably a Distribution Deal, an exclusively exceptional deal that allows the artist to remain the owner of their masters and copyrights while their material is being licensed to the label for x amount of time. That deal is a rare commodity when it comes to the Majors. They will normally avoid taking this road with their talent but will compromise to keep them onboard as well as properly promote their material. Confidence and boldness will take you a long way in this business and you have to fight for want is right and fair.

Chapter 9: DEALS

Understanding How Contracts Work

Understanding contracts can pose to be a difficult assessment to process. Especially if you've never been properly educated on how they affect your career. Contracts from the Major's perspective are usually centered around Record Deals (Recording Contracts), legal agreements that bind the business relationships of record companies; and artists for a certain duration of time or term for profitable obligation. This type of contract is exclusively granted on the contingency of supply and demand, with specific details of the artist being obligated as well as responsible to uphold certain recording standards for that company's success. When an artist exclusively enters into a high-end deal with a record label, the company will typically handle all marketing, pro-motional and distributional work with a guarantee of a larger percentage in the royalties that will be returned from record sales.

NOTES

For me, I understood the formula of going independent because it was the very approach I'd followed before I accepted the majors. I possessed a strong desire of believing that my product would compete on a major scale and it was encoded in my natural design to succeed. I had the courage and heart to declare that my visions would become a reality, all in perfect alignment with my zeal to hustle . Trust me when I say "Independency is not meant for everyone", nor are the majors designed for everyone but if you possess a strong enough desire to succeed, either one could work out in your favor. You have to push yourself to become the very success that you want to be viewed as, never wait on a company to promise you the dream that you've already envisioned for yourself.

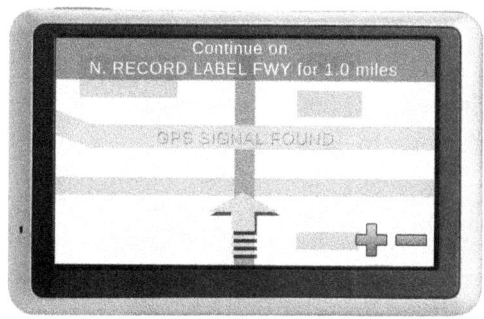

I started young in this Industry and even then I knew there was a benefit of having the freedom to be creative opposed to being told what I could and couldn't create. You have to capitalize on your creativity no matter which route you take. Even when it seems like the window of success is closing on you or your support system is against you, remain who you are and you'll become what you were meant to be. Though your career will go through some major transitions, its clearly up to you to create the outlet that will capture your success as well as sustain it. You must stay wise and if you choose to either go Major or Indie be bold in all of your approaches. This will allow for you to stand out amongst some of the elite that's out there.

As we focus on the INDIE phenomenon that is shifting the infrastructure of the business, we'll learn that it isn't always as easy as it may seem to become a successful INDIE Artist or Label. If you choose to embark on this direction you have to be well prepared mentally to push through the many obstacles that may come your way. Declaring your independency in this business grants you the freedom to operate according to your standards and not from under a corporate umbrella or conglomerate. Keep in mind that with declaring your independency comes great responsibility.

Looking back at the history of the independent approach in the music business we'll find that the indie dynamic has been the very value that the majors were founded on. Every label, artist and professional in the industry starts out independently in some way. With the goal of ultimately being recognized as a commercially successful brand, yet only a few will actually come out as being a successful force in the industry.

Independent record companies usually possess the same characteristics as the Majors but with a few exceptions. Indie's are normally financed by private investors or their owners. This factor alone grants them the power of freedom against the corporate umbrella. They also have their own independent distributors but may use multiple distribution outlets from Majors and privately owned distribution companies as well. Take note that you should always research the independent company's success rate or track record that you are considering to join, just for your own protection.

According to popular culture, to be a affiliated with a Major record company is the most accepted or sought after approach to becoming successful in the music business. There used to be a time when the majors were the only gateway to success but those days have come and gone. With newer formulas being developed from indies everyday, success is clearly reachable even if you haven't joined a Major company or conglomerate. Keep in mind that even established professionals consider leaving the Majors at times, just to explore more creative options.

Though the industry has many record companies and labels, they all possess different organizations and standards that they operate under. Many times in this business, corporate conglomerates will buyout or take over smaller independent labels causing certain infrastructures to change within that label. Take note that you can research some of the majors websites, as they will promote and have constant information on the labels they own or are planning to merge with.

INDIE vs MAJOR

Having a successful career in music is considered to be a reward of the Majors or as referred to in popular culture, having commercial success. Although you may have been promised a guarantee of commercial success once you've taken the major route, this doesn't mean you will become a success in your career or a success for that major company. The Music Industry of today focuses primarily on "The Now" approach of things or as we spoke of earlier in the book, Current Time or what's the latest Trend without any guarantees of instant success. These types of occurrences have left many professionals out of a prosperous career just as quickly as they began. Causing them to take the independent route in order for their careers to even have a chance of survival.

- Artist Development: In Today's Music Industry, this department has diminished or for some companies, no longer exist. This is due to some companies looking at their artists only as products and in most cases this department is considered to be a product development department. Nevertheless, their responsibility is to guide and mold the careers of new artists who are signed under the label, promoting and grooming their image to industry standards or "commercializing" them over the course of their career. Today, those approaches are spent up because the majors want to capitalize from the very beginning of an Artist's career opposed to the long-term approach.

- Publicity Department: This department is responsible for getting the word out about upcoming artists or well known artists. Their job is to make arrangements for articles to be written by magazine companies as well as newspaper outlets, promote radio and TV coverage of artists; and create awareness of everything dealing with that artist's projects. Publicists can also work independently for an Artist as a personal publicist to help coordinate the structure that their company wants to create for that artist.

- Legal Department: The Legal department is responsible for keeping track of all legal documents pertaining to the company and its assets. Every contract that is formed between the company and the artist will be overlooked and documented within this department as well as contracts that the company has established with other businesses etc. This department also manages the claims and lawsuits that may arise against the record company.

- Artistic Image & Design Department: This department is responsible for all art-work, images , photography, CD cover art, designs as well as advertisements and displays that are placed in music stores and promotional outlets.

- Label Liaison: Consisting of one or more people, this department serves as liaison between the label's distribution company and the record company itself, helping decide when a project or album should be released and making sure it doesn't cause a conflict of interest with any other party or label that is associated with or owned by the record company.

- Promotional Affairs: The promotional department's sole purpose is to make sure that the artist or talent that is associated with the record company is being broadcast through multiple media outlets such as radio, video , advertisements etc. This department makes it #1 priority to push the artist's latest material, in order to secure their future success with the company but mainly to ensure the future success of the company, making sure there is clear communication with different departments about the best directional way to sell the artist to the public.

- Production: This department serves as the labels manufacture for all projects associated with the record company. Once the products is completely packaged it is then shipped to the company's distributors who may be apart of the umbrella or a privately owned company. Take note that all majors use major distributors for their products as well as digital distribution.

- Product Management: This department serves as the balance or managerial conglomerate to all the other departments, making sure they stay well ahead of the company's competition and have a clear understanding of the labels needs and policies.

- Business Affairs: Dealing solely with the book keeping, payroll and general finances of the record company, having dealings with foreign licensees as well as having the power to negotiate deals with other executives from other companies.

- New Media: This department works closely with newer aspects of music industry standards, creating a bigger presence for Artists via the Internet, capitalizing on social media outlets using the latest technology to stream songs, performances and music videos to promote the Artists most recent material.

- International Affairs: Consisting of a small group of business execs., this department coordinates the release of projects on a global scale and also works closely with every department within the company.

HOW A MAJOR LABEL IS OPERATED

Major Labels are usually run or are under the complete control of a corporate umbrella or organization called a "Music Group" ,operating itself as an international holding company who also incorporates non-music divisions or sub-divisions, music publishing companies, record manufactures, distributors and labels. These conglomerates control about 80% of the US Music Market and about 70% of the Global Music Market and in time could acquire larger percentages of the entire music market. Major labels have a CEO (chief executive officer) in charge of initial operations within the company as well as a president and vice presidents who are over certain units within the label . The core operations of the majors are broken down into departments that serve as key factors in covering multiple areas of their talent's success.

Let's look into the departments that allow the Majors to Operate successfully;

- A&R: The Artist and Repertoire department is completely in charge of discovering new artists as well as working very closely with the talent they help acquire a contract (deal) for. These individuals do everything in their power to cement the new talent's success by assisting with song selections for their projects, finding award winning producers to guide the project, booking studio time etc., all while being the bridge between the artist and that particular label or company. Keep in mind that some A&R's will give new talent DEMO Deals or Trial Run Deals to test the waters before going full fledge with the Majors.

- Sales: The sales department's primary job is to oversee the complete retail aspect of the record company as well as business. It works very closely with retail outlets, music stores as well as digital retail companies that will distribute and sell the companies product, coordinating these efforts with multiple departments within the record company .

A record label can vary in size as well as status. When a company is considered to be a large international media conglomerate or apart of a large corporate media group they are considered to be a MAJOR LABEL. If they are small in size nor controlled by corporations, practices complex structures within a localized market as well as independently owned, they will be considered to be an INDIE LABEL (Independent Label). In this business you'll come across many individuals posing to be involved in or affiliated with a label. As we stated earlier always stay clear of Phantom Labels (False Record Companies/Imprints), who are scam companies that represents one individual. This notion is often created from the illusional plans of bad representation. If signed to one of these labels, it may be very difficult to get opportunities; reach your full potential or success in your career; as well as prove to be a very damaging process to end the agreement. Keep in mind to always check credentials before agreeing to or signing anything.

In the Music Industry of today there happens to be only 3 Record Labels fully operating as Majors, Universal Music Group (UMG), Sony Music Entertainment (SME) and Warner Music Group (WMG). These corporations play host or are parent companies to a number of SUB-LABELS that trade under an alternate name called IMPRINTS, who normally operate as project units or divisions within the label who operate strictly as a trademark or brand. The Majors also establish VANITY LABELS for certain Artists, carrying the imprint and impression of that particular Artist's control or ownership but it really just represents a standardized relationship between the label and talent. In most cases the Artist only controls the usage of that name as it is part of the label or may possess a little more leverage of their packaging direction but nothing more. Most Artists will establish a label before they sign with a major and this poses as a smart investment that can work for their advantage if the label decides to purchase that imprint .

Chapter 8:
RECORD LABELS

The first thought that comes to the minds of many creative individuals is the urgency to "Get a Deal" or "Get Signed" to a Record Label once they've built up their music repertoire. Without the proper knowledge and understanding the pros and cons of the industry, pursuing the wrong deal blindly could cost you your career. As you've traveled to this point on your journey you now possess the knowledge of what you want to accomplish in the end but before you continue on, lets cover some key factors about record labels.

WHAT A RECORD LABEL REALLY IS

For many, a record label symbolizes a company built on success, super stardom and the ultimate gateway to fame & fortune. Though that may be the illusion that is given about labels, it is really a bit more complex than that. The term Record Label derives from the label placed in the center of a vinyl record that signifies a brand or trademarked company that produces, manufactures, markets and distributes the release of musical works from their stable of artists. These companies can be ran by one individual or a corporate conglomerate of individuals. Record labels possess the power to conduct talent scouting of national and international talent while improving artistic developments with the assistance of A&R's (Artists and Repertoire), who on the behalf of the label maintains contractual/legal agreements between newly discovered talent, detailing the strict enforcement of distinctive obligation.

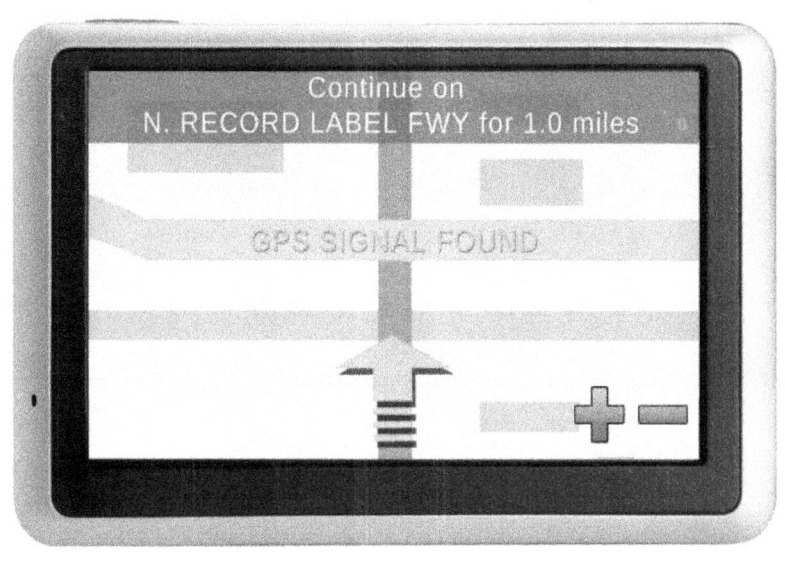

NOTES

Here are the rights you possess as the Copyright Holder and the Royalties they generate;

1. The Right to Copy: Print/ Mechanical Royalties

2. The Right To Distribute: Mechanical/Print/Digital/Synch Royalties

3. The Right to Perform: Performance/Synch Royalties/Digital Royalties etc.):Digital/Synch/Performance/ Royalties

4. The Right to Creatively Enhance Derivative Works (Remix or add Variations): Mechanical/Digital/Synch Royalties

5. The Right to Visually Display (Create Videos, Live Appearances etc.):Digital/Synch/Performance/ Royalties

These exclusively adds power to your success, always protect your material.

Understanding royalties in its entirety has become very complex over the last few years with the consistency of digital innovations in music. That factor alone has caused the format in which royalties stand on to rapidly change drastically. To fully comprehend the way they work will take some time to process. In the next couple of years we'll be introduced to newer, more convenient and secure ways to receive royalties for our creative works with a clear understanding of how we are to track them. Stay patient and you'll begin to reap the benefit of receiving royalties for your musical works.

- Rights Flow: This third party administrator provides the services to license, account as well as pay mechanical royalties. They are usually paid by the licensees such as artists, labels, distributors and online music services and does not extract a commission from the mechanical royalties that were paid out.

- Sound Exchange: Is a non-profit organization that was defined under legislation to act on the behalf of record companies to license performance and reproduction rights, negotiating royalties with the broadcasters. SE is governed by a board of artist and label representatives with services of track level accounting for performances to all of its members as well as the collection and distribution of foreign royalties. SE handles only the collection of royalties from compulsory licenses for non-interactive streaming services that use satellite, cable or internet methods of distributions.

- CARP: The Copyright Arbitration Royalty Panel sets the statutory rates between a Willing Buyer and Willing Sellers in the absence of a voluntary agreement between Sound Exchange and broadcasters.

Everyday new ways are emerging to recover royalties for your musical works, so keep in mind that you should always monitor your royalties and the rights that have generated them.

royalty rate 3-6% or more depending on the project. Publishers usually granted these royalties first due to strict contractual obligations but a single payment may be renegotiable in advance. Take note that it is very important to establish a valid contract or agreement between the publisher and yourself that will be fair.

- Print Royalties: These types of royalties were the first form of musical royalties generated or that applied to music. Deriving from the sales of sheet music for movie scores, compositions and popular songs or tunes around the 18th century and even to-day sheet music is still actively generated sales with a royalty rate of 8-20%(12-14%)

- Digital Rights Royalties: With the growing rate of digital technology overtaking the industry, we are beginning to notice various ways to receive royalties for our work. Digital Rights Royalties derive from simulcasting, web-casting, viral streaming, digital downloading, mobile ring tones and accessing various ON-DEMAND services. The term Digital Music applies mainly to internet and wireless technologies that generates music digitally. These specific music files are identified by serial numbers embedded in the data such as the watermarking or through the natural patterns of a fingerprint within the data. This digital approach has created a different direction within the music industry by capitalizing on the global or international distribution capabilities of instant hearing or storage of music by private and public people. This platform is becoming the predominant form of music but I believe albums and CD's will still survive the digital ages reign.

- The Harry Fox Agency: HFA is considerably a state approved collector serving as the predominant licensor and distributor for mechanical royalties and for its operations and charges 6% as commission. This agency is expected to act in the interests of composers and songwriters and obtains the right to audit record company sales if needed to track down lost royalties.

Here's a breakdown of the main types of royalties you can benefit from in the Music Industry and the Agencies that can assist you with recovering them;

• Mechanical Royalties: Deriving from the sales of recorded music such as CD's, Vinyl Records, MP3 Downloads etc. These royalties are usually paid to artists and publishers by record companies through licensing agencies such as the Harry Fox Agency and the American Mechanical Rights Agency with a royalty rate of 10%-25%. For Recording Artists who don't write, produce and compose their own material, mechanical royalties are the only royalties they'll earn unless they broaden their repertoire.

• Performance Royalties: As we discussed earlier, PRO's are responsible for collecting these types of royalties that are generated from performing, recording or broadcasting live music once they are compensated by broadcasting companies and radio stations who showcase the music. Performance Royalties are usually categorized under two classifications and that is, those associated with conventional forms of music distribution and those associated with digital rights and communication, entertainment and media technologies(Mobile Ring Tones, MP3 Downloads and Live Internet Streaming). Only copyright holders, composers and publishers are entitled to these royalties not recording artists or record companies.

• Synchronization Royalties: SYNCH Royalties also known as SYNCH Licenses ,are generated once musical works or compositions are used in movies, film sound-tracks, television etc., extending into live media performances such as plays or live theatre. Most times there will be a Royalty Free clause within the field of synchronization when music is being used from within a catalogue or library, where a one-time royalty advance has already been paid.

SYNCH Royalties possess a strong practice within the concept of the Laser Drop (Formally known as the Needle Drop), in which the synchronized royalty becomes payable every time the laser drops down on the CD, MP3,WAV or FLAC files of the song in a public performance including every advertisement or commercial associated with the material, every rerun shown by every TV company that has the material,webcasts, media microchips of the content (embedded into karaoke machines, toys etc)., with a

Chapter 7:
ROYALTIES

UNDERSTANDING ROYALTIES

When it comes down to having financial stability for your career in music, earning multiple streams of money will be the major factor for stabilizing your wealth. The main source of revenue that you will earn in this business is Royalties. They will serve as a multiple channel for streaming income within your musical career. Royalties are considered to be private sector tax payments made by certain parties to licensors for the usage of materials or assets for an on going period of time. In music, these royalties are usually linked to songwriters, producers, artists etc., as a percentage of gross or net revenue that derives from fixed pricing over the amount of units sold, generated and digitally transmitted for streams of future royalty payments collectable by the license owners.

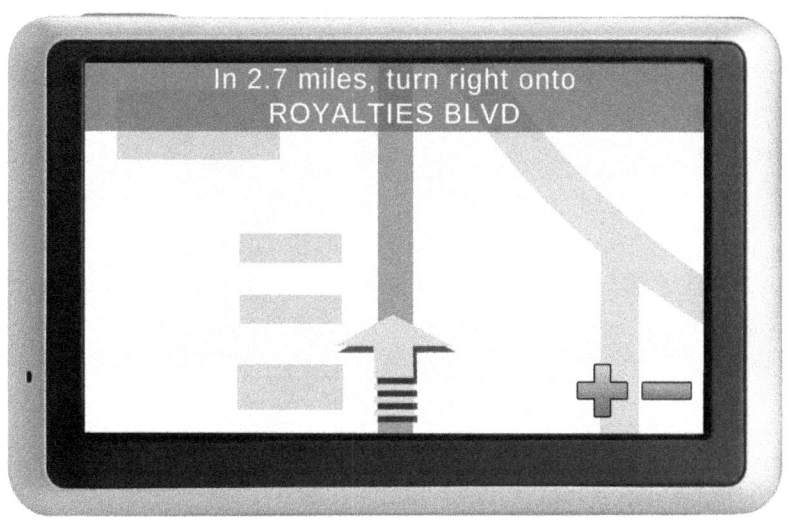

NOTES

frequent usage of a composition or song, for example; ASCAP uses a random sampling method to track down royalties, SESAC utilizes analytical cue sheets for performances and digital outlooks for radio performances, while BMI capitalizes on a more scientific approach to tracking down your royalties . Once these organizations receives payment from the broadcasters and other musical outlets they are solely responsible for compensating you and your publisher. It will be a wise choice to join one of these professionals as they will serve as the bridge between the industry and one of your main sources of musical income, Royalties. Take note that it is very important for you to manage the tracking of your royalties as well just to stay on the safe side of things.

Once you've built yourself a good repertoire of music public performances will be more prevalent in your career. Outside of creating your music you must possess the attributes to perform as well, this allows for you to gain a bigger following and fan-base . Take note that in this industry it's all about building up a prominent following that will play a major role in your future wealth. Performing your music in public can be a tricky task if your just starting out because your not sure how the audience will receive you. This will gradually change the more you showcase yourself.

When it comes to performing your music publicly, you must be the copyright holder or have permission to perform the material. This is for your own protection from legal matters or infringement issues that may add hindrance to your career growth. The term Public Performance means performing your material or live music in a public place. This is as opposed to the recorded version of your work in settings other than around your immediate circle of friends, family etc., on plat-forms such as web broadcastings/streaming, concerts, nightclubs, restaurants, live TV, festivals and radio. Keep in mind that before you agree to these types of performances that your paper work is well taken care of and that your material is protected.

PERFORMING RIGHTS ORGANIZATIONS

Once you have completely packaged your musical works, multiple broadcasters and musical outlets will pay for the use of your music. This is usually done by either getting permission from your label or you; obtaining a license directly from your publisher or they can obtain a license agreement from a PRO (Performing Rights Organization) that grants them permission to use all of the music in their database or repertoire. A PRO , also known as a Performing Rights Society , provides intermediary services of collecting royalties between you as a copyright holder and parties that have used your copyrighted material publicly. In the US we serve as home to the top three PRO's in the business and they are ASCAP (American Society of Composers, Authors and Publishers), BMI (Broadcast Music Incorporated) and SESAC (Society of European Stage Authors and Composers). These PRO's will typically negotiate blanket licenses with radio stations, TV networks and other musical platforms that are granted the right to perform the music they have in their repertoire for a set sum of money. Each one of these PRO's use different methods and formulas to track or determine the

Chapter 6:
PERFORMING RIGHTS

PERFORMING RIGHTS

As we discussed in previous chapters, having the ownership of your copyrights and publishing adds a significant amount of benefits and protection towards your financial success in music. In this chapter we'll be speaking about Performing Rights and how it can be a pivotal source or asset for your success. Performing Rights is a form of copyright law that grants you the right to receive performance royalties for your work. As well as the right to perform or utilize your material in public with demands of payment to you the creator of the works and or the publisher with a 50/50 share or royalty split that is subject to change depending on the contract that you established.

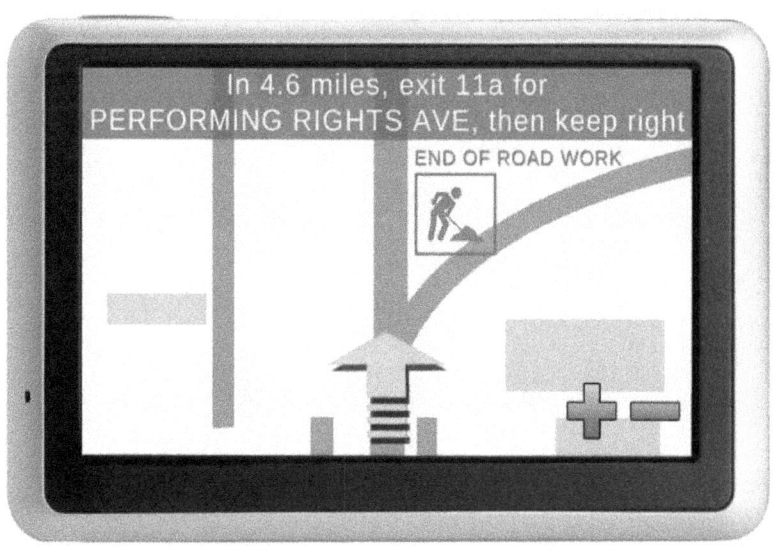

NOTES

This route is often practiced when individuals are going for a global market for their material. Consisting of a team of licensors and marketers who form a partnership with main publishers to push your material in various territories, retaining 10-15% of marked retail pricing of your work as well as remitting the balance back to your main publisher that they share the license with. When your work is licensed out through this type of publisher, they will earn between 15-20% of the share.

Publishing is very important and I believe that when it comes to your musical success that it is the most important step to take care of. Having your material published grants you financial longevity and security for your success in this business. For example; Lets say you created a song that didn't do as well as you thought it would when it was released or was in rotation. Years pass by and that same song has been licensed out by your publisher for a commercial or film etc., By establishing and certifying publishing in the beginning for that material grants you song royalties that can range from high $$$$ to $$$$$$$ in the end. That's the type of power you have with publishing the wealth of longevity.

Here's a few ways that you can establish Publishing in the Music Industry;

1. Self Publish: This independent approach is commonly used by the "IN-DIES" , certifying you as the sole publisher over your works. This can be done by registering yourself or brand as an actual publishing company or sole-proprietorship, acquiring an EIN (Tax Identification Number) for that company solidifying authenticity of your brand. Doing this will grant you the access of joining a PRO (Performing Rights Organization) as a Publisher , keep in mind that you may still join a PRO without being a publisher but note that they are not a publishing company.

2. Publishing Deal : You can build a relationship with a publisher and sign a publishing contract detailing the percentage that they'll receive for issuing your work. Either one of these routes can play out in your favor, even though most successful individuals choose to build a relationship with a publishing company. The reason why some may choose a publisher over self-publishing their works solely falls upon what the publisher is offering to do. Publishers agree to making sure that their clients receive opportunities and royalties from various uses of their material. For example; If you happen to be a songwriter, producer etc., your publisher will work diligently on your behalf to accurately link your songs with the right recording artists to record the material for film/movie soundtracks, TV commercials, album placements etc. The publisher will also provide substantial advances against future income as well as handle copyright registration and ownership matters on your behalf. In return receives a percentage as high as 50% depending on certain types of royalties you receive. Make sure that if you choose to go with a publisher that they work under a certified brand or have certified credentials before you sign any contract with them.

3. Foreign Publishing: Acquiring this form of publishing involves the methods of Sub-Publishing and Co-Publishing.

Chapter 5: PUBLISHING

PUBLISHING BASICS

The Music Industry is more of a battlefield than a stage when it comes to earning money off of your works. If you don't have the proper publishing, you could very well lose the war on earning money in the music business. Just like copyrights, publishing can be a bit intricate to understand as well, especially if you don't have the proper knowledge on how to establish publishing. Once you get over the fear of not knowing what publishing is and how it will benefit your career, you'll start to realize that it becomes simple. For starters, Publishing represents an occupational business or activity that prepares and issues publishable materials such as copyrighted music, books, journals etc., and is how you are able to receive royalties for your work, which we'll discuss in coming chapters.

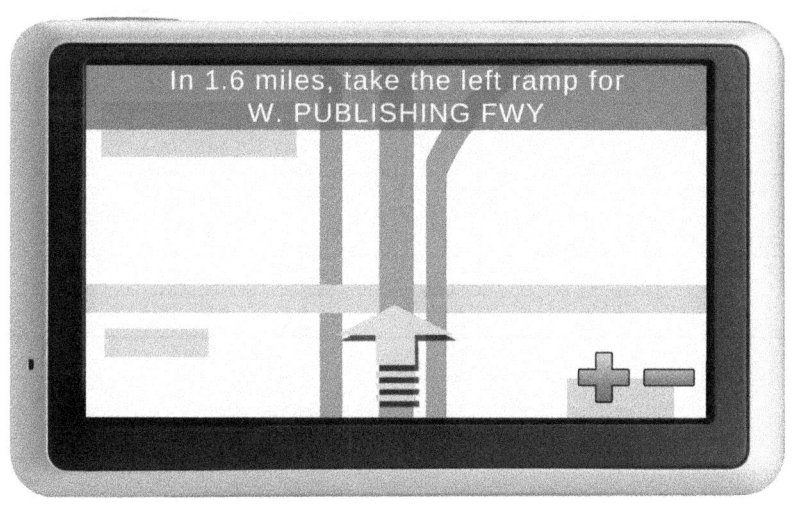

NOTES

We've come to understand that our music is going to make us money and it is up to us to make sure that we take the proper steps, learn the proper education and apply that to securing your financial future. You have in your possession, your copyrighted material which allows you to have the freedom to breathe and create in this industry, without the worry of your property not being stolen.

THE POOR MAN'S COPYRIGHT

Through the years, the music business has seen some weary times and as a result of those hard times comes the inaccurate knowledge surrounding how you are to obtain copyrights if your low on funds. Most commonly is the folklore of the Poor Man's Copyright . This tale has been passed down for generations in the music world and like other tales passed down, people begin to believe in it. The Poor Man's Copyright is considered to be a widely circulated strategy to avoid the fees and overall cost of copyright registration for your material by mailing your created work back to yourself in a sealed envelope by registered mail, using the post mark to establish the filing date of that material. Although through word of mouth you may here others saying they've used this technique and it worked for them or it has worked sufficiently through the years, take note that the Poor Man's technique has not been recognized in any published opinions or doctrine of the United States Court. You must make wise decisions on this journey, by taking the proper steps to protect your artistic creations not the easy road out or shortcut. The United States Copyright Office makes it very clear that this technique is no substitute for your actual registration and will not constitute dispositive proof that the creation enclosed is original nor who actually created it or who the creators were.

Many people in the Music Industry will try to convince you that you really don't need to do anything formal to prove or claim ownership of your creations other than to establish that you originated the work but that would be contradictory to their claim of not doing anything formal. You need to take all proper steps to secure the protection of your material and that means getting your material registered. The sole purpose of copyright registration is to place on record a verifiable account of the date and content of your work, cementing you as the sole copyright holder from an official government source in the event of a legal claim, case of infringement or plagiarism etc. It is very important to obtain federal registration of your copyright with the United States Copyright Office. It's for your protection.

As a copyright holder you have the power to protect a large area of your creative works such as literary works, musical works and most importantly your sound recordings. Though copyright law protect a wide variety of creative works there are some areas that are left out of the protection of your creative works such as titles, slogans, names, ideas, themes, short phrases or concepts. These items require a Trademark in order to be protected, which is another form of legal protection. However, you may copyright and trademark a logo that you associate your brand with. For example; If you go by a stage name or pseudonym in music, it would be wise to trademark that name as your brand, adding more power to the protection that you already have that can go for creative artwork or images that you associate that monicker with.

As new digital media avenues continue to grow throughout the world of entertainment, countless numbers of copyright cases are beginning to soar. This is due to new developments in technology for media downloading outlets and sites that makes it extremely hard to enforce copyright legislation and to stop digital piracy of your creative works. Certain legislations within copyright law date back or over a 100 years and with that being said, it is becoming a very difficult task to protect the creative works of millions of copyright holders within this digital rights age, that we reside in. Usually, there are few limitations to copyright protection but now there are starting and become exceptions to your copyrights or a "Fair Use" exemption towards your material or exclusivity of the copyright that allows users certain rights of a particular material, such as a YouTube digital cover of your work. With the rapid rate of digital piracy and infringement that is shifting the industry's format over the internet, these exemptions are bound to change. Throughout the world of music millions upon millions of copyright holders have pursued and advocated extensions as well as expansion of their intellectual property rights, seeking additional legal as well as technological enforcement over certain media websites that possess their material illegally. As these cases continue you to climb, I believe it would be safe to say we will certainly see a direct revamping of the copyright legislation very soon.

Chapter 4: COPYRIGHTS

Understanding how Copyright Law works can pose to be very complex and intricate at times. In this chapter we'll summarize the most important facts you'll need to know as it pertains to your career in music and the significance it has in your creative success. Please feel free to research in depth the various types of copyright laws.

WHAT IS COPYRIGHT?

A copyright is an exclusive form of legal right given to an originator of creative works granting them the permission to legally print, perform, record, publish and distribute material as well as authorizing others to do the same under legislated law. Copyrights are also considered to be intellectual property and is applicable to any expressive form of information. With your copyrights you possess exclusive rights that only you as the copyright holder are allowed to have for your works and that includes producing electronic copies of your work, create derivative adoptions to your original work, publicly display these works as well as transmit to digital radio and video. Keep in mind that if someone decides to use your material for any purpose that you must make sure you are protected.

The Purpose of Copyrights

The main purpose of this right is to promote the creation of your works by permitting you complete control and profitability for your material or creative works. Once you've obtained the copyrights for your material they are legally upheld for the duration of your lifetime plus an additional 70 years after your death or in some cases in different countries it can extend well up to 100 years after your death.

NOTES

When this is combined with your representation, it can be very detrimental to your career, causing you a lot of unnecessary stress and mental strain. This normally shows if you have a representative who is money driven or only goes after the deals that would be financially beneficial for them or places them in a position of immediate power. Always keep an eye out for representation who want to sign you under "Them" or under a Phantom Label (False Record Company). Remember they work for you not the other way around.

3.   Freeloaders: These are people who take advantage of others generosity without giving anything in return. In your initial team these individuals can be apart of your entourage if you have one or even random people outside of your team such as long lost relatives, or so called friends etc. They only want to use you for your initial gain of success and wealth. Be very careful of who you help out along the way because it may cost you big in the future.

Building up your brand's definition is everything and most importantly marketing your brand's image. You'll begin to realize that in this industry most people strive to be a good product, disregarding the fact that their success could be improved by becoming a better brand. Look at it this way, you can create a successful song but once the success of that record dies down so could your popularity but with a strong brand, your career will be invested into by your fans and followers. Keep in mind that as you continue on this journey that diligently marketing your brand will ultimately pay off in your future.

2.   Business Manager: In the context of the music industry your Business Manager's main job is to supervise all of your business affairs and properly handle your financial matters as well. Making sure you stay on top of personal bills, fees, taxes etc., having a good business manager will keep your financial wealth afloat. The commissioned rate percentage or fee for a business manager is 5% or sometimes an hourly rate, a flat fee or a combination of the two. This is subject to change or increase depending on their credentials. Take note that your Business Manager has to be a CPA(Certified Public Accountant), its very important to financial security and stability of your career.

•   Hitch-Hikers: As we look into the term Hitch-Hiker, we find that it represents a person who travels by getting free rides by passing vehicles. Now this term can relate to your career in a few categories such as business, creative and personal. The industry is filled with individuals looking to get a free ride to their destination and your career may just be their free ride. Avoiding these individuals can sometimes be tricky because they can be close to you and never reveal their true intentions to you.

Here are a few signs/characteristics to look out for that will determine if someone is part of your team or is a "Hitch-Hiker":

1.   Opportunists: People who exploit circumstances to gain immediate advantage rather than being guided by consistent principles or plans. Be very watchful of people on your team who show signs of this characteristic in their behavior or approach to your career.

2.   Greedy Representation: Looking into the word "Greedy", you'll find that it is defined as having or showing an intense and selfish desire for something, such as wealth and power.

the business and guiding your career, just because it sounds cool. If they're allowed, this position could ruin your business ventures and career. Always think smart and do your research to find that worthy individual who will keep your vision and direction ranking first place in this race.

• Creative Advisors: Creative Advisors are individuals who capitalize on your creative direction; enhances your brand and core work. It's always a plus to have a creative team within your initial team. A team of creative advisors could consist of Songwriters, Producers, Musicians, Publicists and Stylists etc. These individuals keep the creativity of your brand moving forward. Keep in mind that adding these pieces to your brand's puzzle will improve your career as well, but you have to make sure that the pieces you incorporate understand who's the captain of the ship. Some may aim to take your vision in their direction or in other lanes, causing you to lose your route and place within the industry. Be very wise with your selection of creative advisors.

• Legal/Financial Advisor: When you finally reach a certain level of success in your career, it would be wise to have legal and financial representation on your team. These individuals will be able to advise you when it comes down to contracts, percentages, licenses, royalties and various legal and financial matters that collectively pertain to your business investments and more.

1. Entertainment Attorney: When it comes down to the legal/business aspect of your music career, an attorney will be able to look over talent agreements, producer agreements, synchronization rights, industry negotiations, contracts, general intellectual property issues and copyright right legislations. Entertainment Attorneys are under a strict confidentiality agreement with their clients with the specifics of their job kept secret, although some E.A's job descriptions have become comparable to agents, managers or publicists. These attorneys are not limited to legal paperwork but rather assist with building your career. Most Entertainment Attorneys charge an hourly rate of $100 and up or a retainer fee but very seldom work on a contingency basis as other attorneys do.

Once your manager has acquired a good business contract etc., their interests as well as obligation incentives are aligned, sharing the interest in your success as well.

As your career begins to soar to higher levels of success your manager's role will become just as important, shifting the guaranteed percentage that you initially agreed upon for their income. Take note that your manager is only entitled to a commission of 15-20% of your Net Income or monies that you've actually collected. Not your Gross In-come or monies that you've earned. Throughout the Music Industry there are a few managers who charge 30% and up but if they don't possess a profitable track record within the business or have established connections that will take your fiscal earnings to the next level, avoid the trap that they're trying to set for you. You have to stay aware of the scam managers in this business. Make sure you always read through the fine print of your agreements or it can cost you big.

3. Agent vs Manager: The roles of these two are becoming more parallel within the business today but there is one important difference to consider before breaking down your decision. In most cases, agents will have the licensing authority to make deals for their clients while managers usually can only establish connections informally with constituents on your behalf forfeiting the power and ability to negotiate contracts on multiple levels. Your brand is priority in your career and your decision will solely come down to who's the most established and well polished representative to help with your vision and career growth.

Remember that when it comes to your career you hold the power above all so in other words, do not allow your representation to take over the vision of your career. In some cases it becomes easy for you to allow your career to become lost within the grasp of your manager or agent. This happens if they've discovered you, have taken over the brunt of your work, have given creative insight towards material landing themselves writing/producer credits, or have a hidden agenda for their own success. Be very careful when choosing this person as well as research their timeline of work or success rate with other clients in the industry and most importantly they have to know about the music business. In other words try not to give this position to relatives, close friends etc., who really don't have a clue about

2. Manager: There are two managerial forces that would be great for your career and that is a Talent Manager and Music Manager.

•   Talent Manager: These managers will guide your professional career in the music industry. Overseeing the everyday business affairs of your brand as well as advising and counseling you when it concerns personal/professional decisions, as well as long term matters etc. that may have an affect on your career. A talent manager can also help or assist you in finding an agent as well as advise you when it would be best for you to leave an agent.

•   Music Manager: This manager's job role takes shape in your career by either being hired by you or in some cases being the person who discovers you as a talent. The relationship that you build with your Music Manager is usually established on a verbal or written contractual basis, with mutual assurances, warranties and profitable guarantees for your future together. Establishing a clear understanding of your brand direction as well as the level you'd want to exceed to. Also handling extensive administrative work within your career such as bookings, promotions, contracts, business deals/ventures etc. This manager usually will solidify all creative developments of your brand before pushing the the focus of concentration towards product development and should be able to handle the bulk of the business load of your career's developmental stage.

Though your manager may carry several loads or wear multiple hats in the development of your career their contract cannot license those responsibilities in the same way that a state license would give empowerment to an agent within your career. Therefore, it would be wise to clarify certain details within the contract to avoid a conflict of interest in the future. Your manager should be able read and understand every angle, explaining in detail the long-term implications of the contractual agreements that you have entered into. Keep in mind that before your manager enters into a contractual agreement with you that their relationship is regarded as *"Competing for Interest"* on your behalf.

Here's a breakdown of those key professionals that can be pivotal in growing your brand as well as evolving your career;

• Representation: As you travel full speed ahead in your career it may become very overwhelming for you if you don't have help guiding your career, this is where an Agent or Manager comes in handy. Although most of the time in the media the reputation of agents or managers are viewed as misrepresenting the careers of their clients or known to take larger percentages of monies from their clients, or has been fraudulent all along with guiding their clients career, despite the turbulence of scams out there having an accredited representative who is a CPA (Certified Public Accountant) will increase your career's potential for successful growth.

The Benefits of having an Agent or Manager

When it comes down to which would be the best representation in upholding the value of your career and brand for the long haul, both could be very beneficial if you're comfortable with their work ethic.

Here are some facts about the two;

1. Agent: The role of an agent is to solely find jobs for clients within the Entertainment Industry or Artists, Actors, Authors, Film Directors, Musicians, Models, Producers, Professional Athletes and Writers. In addition to finding jobs they must also defend, support and promote the interest of their clients while embracing the vision of that client's brand. Possessing accurate knowledge of their clients strengths and weaknesses these agents know exactly how to match their client's with the right companies or businesses. Respectable agents are usually certified and are members of some of the top talent agencies throughout the entertainment world. So if you are thinking of going with an agent you must make sure you research their credentials. Licensed agents are paid a percentage of your gross earnings (typically 10%) and often times operate on regulated terms established by their legal jurisdiction for operation or artist union groups.

- **EXPANSION**: As a brand you need to expand your reach within this industry and beyond. For example; As a music professional you have the key to open major industry doors within Fashion, Filming, Entertainment, Environmental, Philanthropic, Health etc. Take note that you should only pursue expansion if you have a strong enough brand that can globally compete on multiple levels and markets.

Establishing a Branding Package

The music industry of today is filled with individuals who don't have a clue on how to pack-age their brand. Many will have the creative part down but lack the proper packaging steps to take once that process is complete. With a few simple approaches to putting your brand in place you can grasp musical success for the long run. Starting with the basics, if you're an Artist (Rapper, Singer, Producer etc.) you have to polish up your product material and this includes creating commercial quality recordings (Mixed/Mastered,Radio Ready material) that can compete in the industry, create a Press-Kit (Media Kit) which will consist of all of your promotional essentials such as Promo/Sample CD's,Professional Pictures, Bio's, Performance Footage, Merchandise (Shirts,Hats etc.) that can be distributed amongst Promotional Events, Record Label Execs., Talent Agencies and A&R's. Once you've completed those steps your brand will be halfway complete. You have a few more things to tackle like assembling your team or perfecting your image before presenting yourself to the "BIG WIGS" of the music industry.

TEAM

Assembling the perfect team to push your brand forward can be a bit tricky, considering that you'll go through a few trials and errors finding the right people who can trustfully represent you and your brand throughout the industry. This period of your journey is your Carpool Lane. This consists of you adding professional pieces such as Representation (Agents,Management,etc.) Creative Advisors (Writers,Producers etc.) and Legal/Financial (Entertainment Lawyers/Attorneys, Business Managers etc.) to help you on your journey. Keep in mind that traveling with the wrong people down this lane could cost you big in your career, stay alert and protect your career from Hitch-Hikers who will try to take you off of your initial route.

The brand that you'll create for your career direction could lead you down the entrepreneurial road as well. With the likes of Diddy, Jay-Z and P. Miller for example, who went from Rap-Stars to Business Moguls as they acquired a countless number of assets under their belt from Fashion Lines, Record Companies and various retail categories etc. As a brand you control the lane of your success but you also have to be smart about your investments.

What Your Brand Will Consists of:

- **TALENT:** Talent serves as your core attribute on this journey because it's the reason you decided to become a Music Industry Professional. The things you are talented at will multiply once the value of your brand becomes strong, keep in mind that the main thing that strengthens your brand isn't your talent alone.

- **VISION/DIRECTION:** Having a strong vision and direction of the level that you see your brand reaching, you will gradually increase your financial potential on many levels within the music business. Vision is everything, especially in the entertainment world. Your audience and followers have to connect with your vision in order for you to come out as being successful.

- **MATERIAL/PRODUCT:** Now that you've discovered yourself, it's time to present what you have. This consists of Sound Recordings, Press Kits, Merchandise, Song Catalogues, Industry Certification, Knowledgable/Reputable Credentials. Your product and material must uphold quality and reflect promotional assurance that your brand is the number one priority in your career.

- **GOAL:** Though you have an individual or overall goal for your music career, the goals of your brand are considered to be sub-goals or milestones of your career. You must realize as soon as your career is in bloom that you represent your business and your brand showcases your attributes, capital gain and career accomplishments. These things will magnify your track record as well as grant you more opportunities for your future.

Chapter 3: BRAND

As you move forward in your career considering yourself as a Brand will be one of the most important steps that you'll take towards being successful in the music industry. Once you've collectively molded your creativity with your business attributes, your brand will become sculpted into the lanes of multiple industries of the entertainment spectrum. Thinking on a broader scale about your career grants you the willpower to push your vision in various directions and it's solely up to you to be prepared.

Lets narrow down what a brand is and what your brand consists of;

- **BRAND:** Looking into the definition of the word brand we find that it is a certain type of product manufactured by a particular or specific company under a particular name. With being apart of the music business your niche is the product as well as the soul of your particular image and identity. All of your creative endeavors and visions will be regarded as assets to your own career as well as defining your brand. For example; Michael Jordan evolved from being one of the most elite athletes in the NBA to becoming one of the most iconic brands of the 21st century, along with paving the way for a new generation of branding opportunities throughout the world of entertainment. The possibilities of what you'll create as an innovative force for your brand in music are endless. Just look at how super producer Dr. Dre has capitalized on his good ear for music by ushering in the next wave of music listening and beyond with his beats by Dre headphones, marketing them as the must-have headphone system and pushing consumers of the industry to purchase a pair or two.

NOTES

Developing a routine for your career goals while balancing them with your everyday life can serve to be very helpful in your growth as a a professional. Again, this Industry isn't built for the weak and it can become overwhelming along your journey but with a balance it won't be as bad.

GOT TALENT?

As we look closely into the creative spectrum of the music business we can identify with the main ingredient that most creative individuals possess, which is TALENT. Being considered talented amongst the elite in this industry is what gets you the recognition from major companies throughout the business. You may not always get discovered off of your strong suit or niche, you could very well find success within other things that you're talented at. For example, If you're a Singer, Rapper, Performer etc., it may take you longer to really break down the walls to grab the attention of the elites in the business. Especially when there is a multitude of creative individuals that possess alternative gifts. It's going to take for you to add some more tools under your belt to compete in an industry of triple threats or more.

Here is a tip on having a spare (backup talent) if the journey begins to wear your tires (talent) out before you reach your destination.

- **HIDDEN TALENT:** Discover and develop hidden talents about yourself that can become incorporated into your repertoire such as Song writing, Producing, Acting etc. As a creative force it is very important for you to be more than just a one-track or one direction talent in this industry and you must cover all angles and ends of your gift. While finding your niche try equally working on your alternatives and creating a talent balance so that when it comes to presenting who you are, you will be more than what they'd bargained for.

We live in a world where an individual can become iconic in a short period of time if they work hard enough. The reason certain individuals who have become iconically relevant throughout their career is a direct result of them gradually pushing themselves above the grid, ultimately defining trendsetting. The axis that the musical world spins on is not equivalent to that of the real world. Learning this musical rotation can give you an edge on this industry's trendsetting opportunities being it changes so rapidly. Once you've found yourself within your art, it is possible that you'll be the axis the industry decides to spin on so keep in mind this will only occur when you are unique enough to boldly be yourself.

Mastering your niche will be a very pivotal time in your career development. While everyone else decides to stick to following the same simple idea of being the same, you can daringly push to defy greater. For myself, I knew that eventually my own path would lead to greater levels of my gift. We must realize that this industry will embrace our unique approaches but only if we continue to push ourselves beyond the trend as geniuses and set them.

Here are few tips to help you fuel up your niche, mastering its potential;

- **HARD WORK:** Although in today's world this term is said very commonly, hard work really does pay off. The music industry is in dire need of candidates like yourself, you have to be over prepared before your arrival to successfully manage the constant evolution of the music industry. Pushing yourself beyond the normality of yourself creatively has to be your mindset in order for you to succeed. You will endure the fruits of your labor if you keep striving for greatness in your career.

- **BALANCE:** The tapestry of success has its many vices but the key to avoiding those tempting gains comes solely from you creating a balance for yourself.

niche in your career. To obtain that level of skill comes solely from molding and polishing the skills that you already possess. With dedication your diligence will prove to be the formula that you've been aiming to discover. The old saying "Hard Work Pays Off" should be your motto on this journey because it serves as a bridge between your success and your failure in the industry.

Once you've discovered the greatness within your niche you must remain loyal to your aspirations. Working on your mental strength, tolerance and endurance can prove to be very rewarding while pushing for longevity in your career. For example; When we analyze the characteristics of elite athletes such as Competitors, Champions as well as Olympic Gold Medalists etc., we instantly acknowledge their training discipline. These athletes vigorously train themselves year round, evolving and pushing their endurance to extreme levels just to stay well ahead of their competition. When it comes to this Industry, music is your sport and only the strong and skilled will become great. As an aspiring music professional you have to train as well as push yourself to stay ahead of your competition on a multitude of levels , including creatively, mentally, legally and physically. In this business the best way to conquer and defeat your competition is to capitalize on your strengths. This would be considered an element of surprise since the competition isn't looking for you to utilize those tools in your arsenal for success. Keep in mind that your mental strength enhances your self-confidence, you have to boldly be yourself to survive in this business *Niche Mastering*.

For many, the main problem with mastering your niche is the duration of time it takes. This alone causes many who are aspiring to become successful to give up. Especially if it takes years of redefining and construction to actually find their place in the industry. For example; Many aspiring professionals such as Artists, forfeit their true potential more than any other music industry professional. This is mainly due to the creative format of music being aligned on the grid of "Current Time" , not to mention that there is an array of other candidates fighting for their position in popular culture. If we look closely at the current infrastructure for the Artist of today's Music Industry, we clearly notice only a hand full of Artists who actually defy the grid of "Current Time".

Chapter 2: NICHE

Throughout your career you'll be faced with many challenges and most of them will come from within yourself. The main obstacle you'll strive to overcome is finding your niche in this industry. When we analyze the details of this route we learn that the journey to knowing where we stand is never as easy as we presumed. The Music Industry is constantly changing with a growing rate of the few and proud who have found their niche, causing the level of intimidation to soar sky high. This is mainly due to the overwhelming amount of competitors that arises every second, pushing many to lose sight of their game plans and give up from fear. Keep in mind that the Music Business is a very competitive field to pursue and like mixed martial arts the competition is always out for blood. You have to remain strong in this race, your career's survival depends on it.

As it comes down to gradually finding your place in this business, the formula is quite simple. So what is this formula to gradually finding your Niche? I believe that the formula is solely within ourselves and heres why;

As we travel along the intricate roads of the music world, timely searching the ends of the Earth to find that secret formula to owning and developing our niche, we all can agree that there are NO DETOURS or SHORTCUTS to developing this attribute. However, being this exploration will be considered your life's work finding what you're good at isn't the hard part. The hard part is transforming the "GOOD AT" aspect into a "GREAT AT" aspect, taking the evolution of that and respectfully grasping an even "GREATER" niche in your career. To obtain that level of skill comes solely from molding and polishing the skills that you already possess. With a dedication your diligence will prove to be the formula that you've been aiming to discover. The old saying "Hard Work Pays Off" should be your

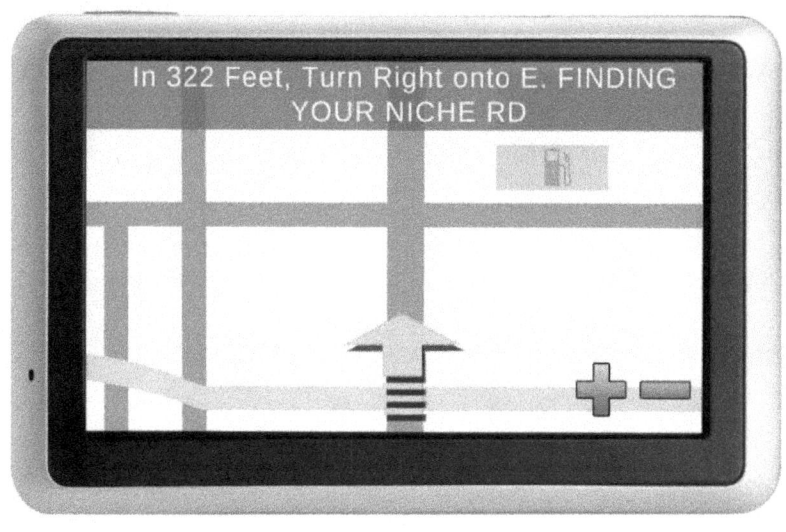

NOTES

- **Passion:** To have passion for your dream and career is very pivotal for your innovative growth. This emotive feeling can enhance your gifts and aspirations, pulling you into a higher level of genius if allowed. Having a passionate approach to your career could grant you favor for the long haul that's ahead of you in the music business. Always allow this attribute to soar to greater heights.

Though there are many options and routes that you could explore always be yourself no matter the route you choose. Your hard work and passion will pay off if you stay driven and focused.

When choosing the best directive route in your career you have to stay focused and determined to succeed in knowing that you've made the right choice. I knew that the path I'd chosen was the right path for my life because of how natural it felt to me. Everything I did became as accurate as second nature. You'll know that its right when you can travel through your career with a purpose of holding your head high doing what you love, which is Music. That outlook was all of the confirmation I needed to continue to strive for success and evolve my musical career. The road of my musical journey was never paved with arrogance or greed but with truth. Success can mean a multitude of things for many but never let your dream be deferred by things of a materialistic value. For example; Don't waist your signing bonus or earned monies on investments that may cause you to lose more than you've actually gained. In this industry you have to remain wise about your spending habits or you'll end up back to the leveled grounds or point in which you first began your journey.

Here are a few key attributes you should consider fueling up on before narrowing down your approach or route;

- **Confidence:** When you are confident in your ambitions as well as your craft, it will strengthen you along your journey to success. This attribute will push you to go beyond your ordinary self to achieve greatness in your career.

- **Belief:** Believing in yourself will uplift your morale as well as fuel your confidence. When you daringly believe in your dreams you will ultimately succeed in anything that you go after. With the power of believing that your gift and craft has the potential to innovate and inspire will grant you the perfect opportunity of becoming iconic.

When we look at how this can relate to the Music Industry, we learn that we serve as that vehicle in our careers. There will always be others who are traveling down the same path and the lanes tend to become a bit crowded. This would cause anyone to change their lane or even try an alternate route. Keep in mind that alternate routes may cause you to lose time to your goals. There is always going to be other aspiring individuals doing what you do or mimicking what you bring to the table. You must remain creative, this allows for you to avoid the heavy traffic which in this industry is constant.

- **Road Blocks:** Road blocks can occur on your road to success in the music industry at any given moment and time. These can consist of Poor Record Sales, Missing Project Deadlines, Dead-End Deals, Unexpected Losses etc. When this occurs you have to remain humble and calm to get through this rough patch in your career.

- **Construction Zones:** We all dread the days when we're hit with construction on our normal route. With these construction zones there's no guarantee that your path will be cleared for you to resume your journey in a pleasant time. In the Music Industry, construction can cause things and plans to be pushed back such as Albums/Projects, Tours and even Debut Appearances. Even though it sounds bad when we think about it or the plans of goals that we want completed on our agenda, it isn't always a hindrance to face construction in your career. Construction is commonly used to breakdown, repair and build up. As it comes to a career in music you'll become very familiar with breaking down and building your career back up on many stages on your journey. It's all apart of the process of finding your place in music successfully. Keep in mind that if you're an Artist etc, you'll face a construction season almost 90% of your career. This is due to the rapid pace that the industry changes at amongst popular culture.

- **Accidents:** In the Music Industry, accidents can and will happen if your not careful with managing your career. Accidents can consist of Publishing/Copyright Faults, Licensing Troubles, Financial Negligence, Poor Contracts, Tax Issues, Sample Clearing Issues, Lawsuits and even Acts of Defamation. All the above can and will injure or kill your success for your career. It would be wise to have a trusted team of advisors and lawyers who have your best interest to stay on top of these issues and watch out for any

- **ROUTE 3** (Financial/Legal): This route is often looked over or rather less pursued than the other two routes. It becomes ideal for aspiring Entertainment Lawyers, Financial Managers, Accountants etc., for they are the individuals who oversee everything legal and profitable within your music. Pursuing this route can prove to be both profitable and time consuming, you have to be mentally prepared for this trip.

In this chapter we'll introduce several new terms that you can use towards understanding this industry as it relates to your journey. The Music Industry today is filled with a wide array of roads and routes that one could choose from. Alluding more than several multi-million dollar dreams for aspiring professionals, choosing the most profitable route would be ideal but not as easy as it may seem. The intricate complexities of the business can leave you lost and scratching your head if the route you choose isn't what you bargained for. It's very important that you research all lanes and routes of the profession you desire to travel along. Though it looks and seems calm from a distance, it may be filled with ditches, heavy traffic, road blocks, construction zones and even accidents.

Lets take a look into these new terms and how they will be more relatable as you progress in your journey;

- **Ditches:** When you think of the word ditch, you usually visualize some uneasy gravel that may be off or alongside of a highway that you wouldn't want your vehicle ending up in. Now when it comes to the industry we can use this term as well. When embarking on a successful career you would want to stay away from ditches, For example; Bad Management, Poor Financial Advisors, Bad Marketing, Promotion, etc.

- **Heavy Traffic:** We all have been on freeways or traveling along the highways in a timely fashion when suddenly, we're plagued with heavy traffic. While this is happening we're wondering where did all these people come from and why did they choose the route we took at that specific time. Unfortunately, there is no cure for heavy traffic but there is always an alternate route.

Chapter 1:
CHOOSE YOUR ROUTE

Before you embark on your journey through a career in music you must first determine which route you are willing to travel down. There are three main approachable routes that you can pursue in the music industry, lets narrow down the path that is right for you.

Below are the top three routes that are commonly taken;

- **ROUTE 1 (Creative):** This route is often traveled by Artists, Songwriters, Producers, Musicians, Sound Engineers, DJ's, Composers, Rappers etc. It's one of the most commonly traveled routes in this Industry. The creative approach has its advantages as well as disadvantages. It has made stars out of many, stirred the controversy of plenty and has also catapulted the legacies of some of the most iconic personalities that the world has ever seen.

- **ROUTE 2 (Business):** This route is often chosen by individuals pursuing the core administration of the business, aspiring to build and mold a creative infrastructure of the industry. From Talent Agents and A&R Executives guiding the careers of Artists to elite powerhouse Moguls ushering in the musical outlets of the next generation, when it comes to traveling along this route you have to be equipped with endurance for the long haul.

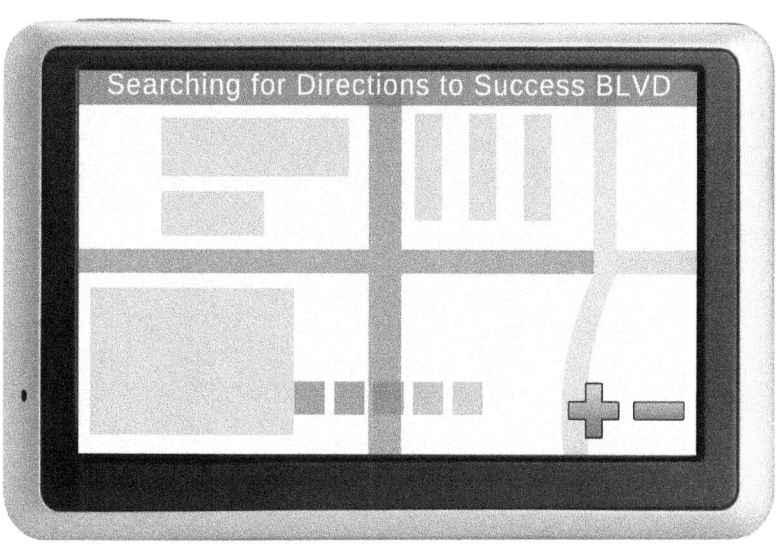

"The Mind Gives us Dreams to see thru to completion. It's up to us to Choose the right route or path for our Destiny to remain True" - Silkk "The Shocker" Miller

The lack of proper information would drive anyone to change their route. Often, some will deliberately misinform you with inaccurate information with a main objective to leave you without an alternate route to take. You would have no other choice but to give up or give in. I believe anyone have the ability to succeed in this business but only with accurate information. You have to be equipped with an arsenal of knowledge to gain leverage in this race. The knowledge of this industry has been recycled in various ways, yet never has pushed the mold to really grant you accurate success or complete result." After researching numerous books, attending music seminars etc., Silkk found that the majority were giving the same thing or the same dull experience. A prelude of "Hype" and more time spent on the visual illusion of helping people obtain great results in their careers. "With this book, I wanted to grant inquiring minds the answers to those questions about the industry that's often asked while they found their place in success. The information that is within this book will help many individuals find success and ease the burdens of this business" states Miller. In this mindfully crafted book you'll be granted a look inside this industry from a personal approach, overcome any stigma on your road to success and grasp any goal you have for your career. "When I was starting out I didn't have a blueprint or a guideline to lead me in the right direction, I had to learn it for myself. I believe that writing this book was very necessary and long over due".

Within the modern pool of the music industry, a large majority of aspiring professionals are swimming towards information or literature about the Music Industry from people or constituents who aren't apart of the business or may not have the proper experience or credentials to give you solutions on such a matter. "No one wants to be given criticism or learn the ropes about their field from someone who's only had a glimpse of what the Industry is really about. Your career should be molded and nurtured to its fullest potential, so you have to be wise about who you give the privilege of educing your career" states Silkk. We've all seen the many approaches to succeeding in the business but PAVED will rejuvenate the careers and the ambitions of millions for the next generation of entertainment success.

Often when Silkk would be asked the reasoning or even the inspiration behind him creating this book, his reply would be, "I simply wanted to inform those who are lacking the proper knowledge and education of the Music Industry. For most people, gaining knowledge about the business in general is usually a 'Learn As You Go' type of arrangement that is commonly practiced by either studying under a professional as an intern, apprentice or just observing certain angles on an individual basis, even that can become an endless maze to follow. Many hope to gain as much knowledge on such an overwhelming career path. Ultimately having the desire to acquire this knowledge in a timely manner." Silkk emphasizes on the fact that this industry requires hard work, diligence and knowledge to push from a Creative Innovator into a Business Exec. "Lets face it, No one wants their career to near its end before they've finally found confidence in the knowledge they have gathered towards succeeding in their career."

PAVED in depth will grant a bird's eye view for those who are in search of a successful direction or route within the music industry. Ultimately, minimizing your obstacles will grant you success. If there was a minimal amount of let downs that may arise to sway you from reaching your goals, your success ratio would continue to grow and prominence would be guaranteed. In this business, the ratio or percentage of being confronted with obstacles is almost 99%-100% but that doesn't mean you won't prevail or succeed in this industry. Although many paths of gain or success come with a price, your situation doesn't have to become more than you bargained for. There will always be an obstacle of road blocks near or detours trying to alter your goals but the key to overcoming the obstacles is solely within your drive and determination. You have to remain driven when faced with adversity in your career. Its the only way you'll make it through this industry. "I've experienced a countless array of obstacles within my career but as I gained the proper knowledge, I persevered. I had to come to the realization that my frustrations towards my goals were caused by certain paths of misinformation.

Introduction

As we look into the complexities of how to effectively become successful in the Music Industry, we will find that most of the standard formulas for acquiring success has become nothing more than an overwhelming stigma for many aspiring professionals. Though the current infrastructure of the business has been heavily guarded by some of the most brilliant minds this industry has seen, the knowledge of their success is no longer hidden in mystery. The road to success will now be within the palms of your hands as Silkk Miller also known as Silkk "The Shocker" Miller has researched the ins and outs of this industry, its countless success stories as well as downfalls of some of the elite in this business, to collectively present this guide to help you find success and have a clearer path for longevity within your career. Creating a unique formula that even the most advanced professional could use, PAVED changes the way people succeed in music.

SILKK "THE SHOCKER" MILLER

PAVED

THE COMPLETE NAVIGATED GUIDE TO SUCCEED IN THE MUSIC INDUSTRY

**PAVED: The Complete Navigated Guide to Succeed
in the Music Industry**

Copyright © 2017 by Silkk Miller
All Rights Reserved. No part of this book may be used or reproduced in any manner whatsoever without prior written permission except in the case of brief quotations embodied in critical articles or reviews.

ISBN: 978-0-9891732-2-3

Visit our website at:
www.pavedbook.com

First Edition
9 8 7 6 5 4 3 2 1

Printed in the United States

www.ingramcontent.com/pod-product-compliance
Lightning Source LLC
Chambersburg PA
CBHW071358160426
42811CB00111B/2221/J